DOMINATE YOUR DEBT

DOMINATE YOUR DEBT

take control. owe less. live more.

Rebecca Eve Selkowe

To Kristin —
Let's Rock this!!!
(and thank you!!!)
Rebecca

vivace media llc

New York, New York

Vivace Media LLC
New York, New York
Printed in New Hampshire

First Edition

Library of Congress Cataloging-in-Publication Data available upon request
ISBN: 978-0-692-59190-1

Book design by Bryn Bachman. www.brynbachman.com
Additional design services by Fyfe Design. www.fyfe.com
Back cover photo by Michelle Kinney Photography. www.michellekinneyphotography.com

....

A ma très chère Mémé Yvette.
Everything that I am, that this book is, could never have been without you.
Je t'aime beaucoup, beaucoup, beaucoup.

....

Table of Contents

Introduction

The title of this book is *Dominate Your Debt*. I chose the word *dominate* because it's a big freaking word, dominating your debt is a big freaking deal, and because frankly, dominating your debt is the only way to deal with it successfully.

The subtitle of this book is equally as important, as it tells you what it really means to dominate your debt: *Take Control, Owe Less,* and *Live More*. It's not just about paying it off; it's about doing it on your terms. It's about feeling powerful and confident. And it's about relaxing because you know with absolute certainty what you need to do and exactly how you're going to do it.

How This Book is Different

Most "how to be good with money" books do not deal directly with debt. You'll find it in a chapter or two, but it's rarely the main focus. The more deeply involved I become in the financial lives of my coaching clients, the more curious I find this. My clients aren't worried about money. They are worried about the *lack of money*. They read financial self-help books and get nowhere because most books are trying to teach things no one needs to know. If you're seeking refuge in the financial self-help section, you aren't trying to learn. You're trying to solve a problem. And the problem you're trying to solve isn't "I don't know enough about money." The problem is "I have debt and I don't feel in control of it."

This book is about solving that problem. Period.

Not only is the subject matter unique, my approach is too. A lot of financial advice falls into one of two camps.

One is the preachy camp. "You don't know any better, so I'm here to school you." This camp is bursting with finger-wags and jam-packed with dry information. Your biggest takeaway is how much you don't know, and you feel judged and defeated before you even try to implement any of it.

The other is the touchy-feely camp. You will feel good in this camp. You will be wrapped in the soft, warm nest of loving your money, saying affirmations, living a rich life, and manifesting your desires. Delicious, gooey, lick-your-fingers advice that is so yummy when you're reading it, you forget that you still haven't figured out what to do with your numbers.

This book falls into both camps and neither of them. There's plenty of warmth and fuzziness in these pages. There is also lot of information and number-crunching, because you need to know certain things that no one is telling you, and because *money is about numbers.*

If you feel preached-to here, I've totally missed the mark. While I believe in a few black-and-white, hard-and-fast, no-effing-around rules, dominating your debt is about so much more than rules. It's about confidence, comfort, and authenticity—feeling like what you're doing and how you're doing it is the right thing for *you.*

I have a lot of opinions, and of course I want you to listen to me and do what I say. But in doing this work with my amazing clients, and having been there myself, I know that the greatest success comes when you develop the ability to listen to *yourself.* I want you to get really clear on what's best for you, and then use the tools I give you to make it happen. Not because I said so, but because you *want* to.

The book you're holding in your hands blends the left-brained numbers, organization, and analysis stuff with the right-brained, soft and squishy, look-inside-and-love-your-money stuff. The goal here is to help you find solutions. Although we may never meet, you've got me in your corner. I will hold your hand, kick your bum, and cheer you the heck on. We're going to have a good time, you and I.

What This Book is About

This book is about empowerment. It is about giving you a framework to understand *your* situation, getting you clear on what feels right for *you*, and creating the space to make it happen—right here in these pages.

This book is designed to be interactive. This book is designed to be *the* debt-dominating resource for you. This book is designed to actually help you take control of your debt, get out, stay out, *and be excited about it.* The work you do in this book will become your playbook for paying off your debt, and you'll never feel sh*tty reading another "Big Money Mistakes You Made In Your 20s" article on the internet. How cool is that?!

Why I Know What I'm Talking About

I own a women's financial education and coaching company. I'm not a talking head, a financial blogger, or a journalist. I'm not on TV offering general "be good with money" advice to the masses. I don't have a financial planning business where I get paid by investors or banks and do this financial literacy stuff on the side. I don't help people file for bankruptcy.

The book that you have here? *Take Control, Owe Less,* and *Live More*? This is it. This is what I help women do.

I started doing this work before I even realized I was doing this work. Growing up, I was always "good" with money. I earned it, tracked it, and saved it. I asked for a cash drawer for Christmas one year and religiously counted and recorded every dollar and coin that went into and came out of it. After college, I got a job as a legal assistant, moved to New York City, started collecting a regular paycheck too large to fit in a cash drawer, and graduated to spreadsheets.

I took out loans when I went to college, consolidated them when I graduated, and didn't really think much about them. At the time, the interest rate on my savings account was 5% (yes, 5%—not a typo!), the interest on my loans was 3.5%, and my minimum payment was $162 a month.

But then—oh, but then!—I decided to go to law school. All the money I had saved during my two years as a legal assistant went toward paying tuition, and I even had a small scholarship. All that together wasn't enough to cover the first year. So, like most students, I applied for and was given "financial aid" in the form of student loans. Big, fat, five-figure student loans, disbursed every semester so I could pay tuition, rent, and living expenses.

While in school, I was getting the loan statements in the mail each month, but I wasn't thinking much about them. "This will be no problem! No problem at all!" I told myself. "I'll be making plenty of money, so there's nothing to worry about."

My student loans went into repayment, as student loans often do, within six months of graduation, and I finally took a good look at the statements.

I was sick.

"How can this be? This can't be real. There must be a mistake." Outraged, I called the loan company. Then I did the math myself. There was no mistake. I owed almost $168,000, and my minimum monthly payment was over $1,700.

To make a long story very, very short, I knocked out my debt in five years. It took a *lot* of work, determination, and discipline. There were many tears, a lot of anxiety, and a trip to a gastroenterologist for stress-related digestive issues.

But I did it.

During that time, I did a ton of research, created a ton of spreadsheets, and had a ton of conversations with a ton of women about money. I was *obsessed* with my debt, and I was fascinated by how different my approach and understanding seemed to be from everyone else's. Hardly anyone seemed to be doing what I was doing or to know what I knew.

Most people accept debt as a fact of life. I don't. Yes, my debt served its purpose. It got me to where I am today, and I'm a better person for it. I wouldn't have become a lawyer if it weren't for the availability of student loans.

And yet. I can tell you, from having been on both sides of the ridiculous and seemingly-insurmountable debt fence, that while debt isn't necessarily to be avoided, it needs to be treated with respect and a heavy dose of reality. That was an incredibly difficult lesson for me to learn, and I learned it the hard way. Learning it made all the difference not just in what I did, but how it *felt* to be in debt. Everything shifted from the day I took control and became determined to owe less and live more.

I want that shift for you, too.

The workouts, information, and advice you're holding in your hands are based on my own personal experience and years of working one-on-one and in groups with dozens and dozens of women. As a lawyer, I am a trained problem-solver. As a financial coach, I get my fingers all up in my clients' finances, and together we figure out what's working, what isn't, what needs to happen, and how to get it done. And then they do it. This process has been tested, tweaked, challenged, and applied with overwhelming success by real live humans. There's no quick fix, but there is a solution.

My clients have boosted their credit scores by hundreds of points, paid off thousands and tens of thousands and hundreds of thousands in debt, built up tens of thousands in savings, and started their first retirement accounts. These women go from anxious and overwhelmed to savvy and confident about money—and they aren't leading lives of sacrifice and deprivation. They've taken control of their finances and in so doing created the space to chase their dreams, have the things they love, and live with a greater sense of purpose and ease.

Do my clients get stuck along the way? Did I get stuck along the way? Oh, hell yes. But as I and my clients can tell you, what's waiting on the other side is pretty dang amazing. At the risk of sounding incredibly cheesy, you already have everything you need to succeed; it's just a question of unearthing it. You *don't* suck with money. You *haven't* messed up. You *can* do this. And I'm here to show you how. If you do the work—and I mean really dig deep and *do the work*—you can make it happen, too.

How to Use This Book

Why Dominate?

I want to be clear: there is nothing inherently wrong with debt. It plays an important role in our economy, keeps banks, credit card companies, and retailers in business, and even keeps the world economy humming along. Debt is not fundamentally bad. What *is* bad is being in debt and having no informed, clear, realistic plan to get out.

Debt keeps you from being in control. Dominating your debt is about reclaiming that control. Debt + No Plan = Your Lender Taking Over as the Driver of Your Train. It's so easy to sit back and be the passenger. But if you leave the driving to your debt for too long, it can and will take you on detours to places you don't want to go.

Debt keeps you from being free. And this, my lovely, *this* is probably the sneakiest, creepiest thing about debt. It makes you feel free for a time, because it gives you the opportunity to do / be / have things you otherwise wouldn't. But the price you pay is losing control over what happens next.

It's hard, because society isn't exactly trying to help you out. Credit card companies send you piles of offers in the mail, colleges and graduate schools award loans like they're prizes, and everyone seems to want to give you money *now* on the tiny promise that you'll pay it back *later*.

Dominating your debt is grounded in the premise that you deserve to be free and in control. You must believe that you can pay off your debt—it's merely a question of when, and *you* get to be the one to answer that.

The Money Pyramid

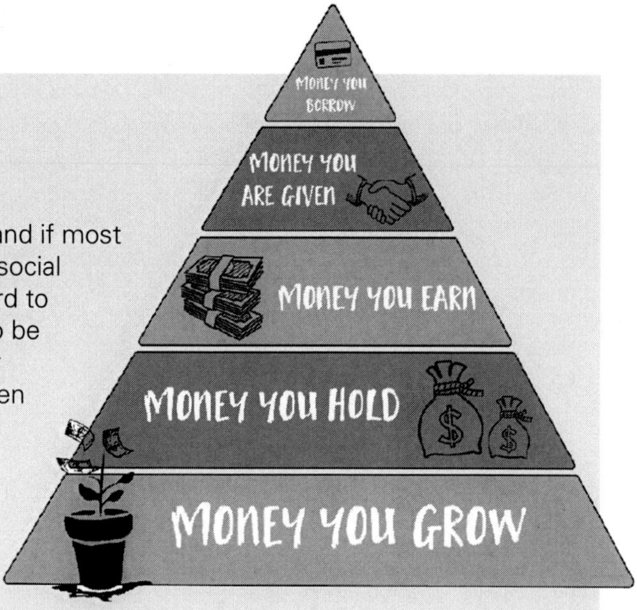

If you've had debt for a long time, and if most of the people in your family and/or social circle are also in debt, it may be hard to imagine a life without it. It may also be hard to put your finger on why your debt makes you feel so uneasy when everyone around you seems to be just fine with it. But when you know, you know.

MONEY YOU BORROW
MONEY YOU ARE GIVEN
MONEY YOU EARN
MONEY YOU HOLD
MONEY YOU GROW

This money pyramid illustrates how debt keeps you from feeling in control.

Money falls into one of five categories:

1. **Money you borrow** (credit cards not paid in full, loans) ⇨ No control. You have to pay it back, plus it's someone else's money.

2. **Money you are given** (gifts, awards, lottery winnings) ⇨ Little control. It's inconsistent and unreliable.

3. **Money you earn** (salary) ⇨ Some control. It still depends on the success of another business and/or a client's or employer's ability to pay.

4. **Money you hold** (savings) ⇨ Full control. It's there until you use it.

5. **Money you grow** (investments, interest) ⇨ Bonus control! You can decide where and how to invest it, and if done well, money creates new money all on its own.

When a pyramid is upside down, it will teeter and spin like a top. Similarly, when your money pyramid is upside down—that is, when the majority of the money you use day to day is borrowed—you are also going to teeter and spin. You may even have gotten quite adept at spinning. But you're not going to feel in control.

On the other hand, when the bulk of your money is in investments and savings, you have the most control over how and where you can get it when you need it, which consequently makes you feel the most free because it's coming from you. You are independent and your financial house is built on a solid foundation.

Once you have debt, there are four ways to get rid of it:

1. Pay it off.
2. Get it forgiven.
3. Declare bankruptcy (note that not all types of debt will go away this way).
4. Die (note that not all types of debt will go away this way).

Taking control of your debt means paying it off on the terms that make sense given your priorities *and* that cost you the least amount of money. It may feel like the less you pay, the more control you retain, but that's not the case. Having debt costs you money, time, and freedom. The longer you have it, the more of those three things it costs you.

The solution, however, is not "get out of debt as fast as possible." The solution is "create a plan that actually makes sense to *me* and then do everything in my power to make it happen." Feeling kickass amazing, like you've accomplished something huge, like you've *dominated your debt*, means recognizing and owning your power in the face of your debt, creating a plan to pay it off, and then sticking to that plan. When you sally forth and attack your debt without a plan, you will start to hate it, and you're likely to find yourself in one of the two following situations.

One, you cut back drastically on your spending, make double and triple payments, and yet never really feel like you are making a dent. You get discouraged. You give up. Ultimately, you resign yourself to the notion that being in debt is just an inevitable part of life.

Two, you get into what I call the Stinky Cycle of Debt. If you've been in it, you know what I'm talking about. You get angry at your debt and throw all the money you have at it. You pay it off quickly. This leaves you with no debt (hooray!), but also no money. Eventually something comes up, you don't have the money to pay for it, and debt slowly creeps up on you again. The Stinky Cycle continues.

Paying off your debt as fast as possible is not a surefire way of getting rid of it for good. Neither is neglecting it and hoping or assuming it will go away.

You need a plan. Together, we are going to create one.

The Steps

So enough talk… let's do this. This book is laid out in sections and is designed to have you take action in each section, in order. It's your party, so you can skip around if you want to, but you will get the most out of it if you go in order.

There are six steps to dominating your debt. Each of these steps involves bite-sized, actionable pieces, deep introspection, and attention to detail. Here we go!

Step One: Educate. When pressed, most people are surprised by how little they know about the details of their debt. If that's you, it is *absolutely okay*. I'll spare you my long and winding rant about how our schools, parents, government, and society are all failing us and sum up with this: the information isn't easy to find, "how debt works" isn't a titillating topic, and there is nothing wrong with you. Just don't be lulled into thinking it doesn't matter. It *does* matter. Things no one bothered to tell you about your debt are majorly affecting your ability to dominate it. This chapter will school you on them.

Step Two: Set Goals. Once you understand your debt, it's time to understand yourself. Reading about how your debt works may well have you seeing red and ready to jump headfirst into a plan. I can't overstate this: you *must* do a thorough exploration of the inner-game stuff—your motivations, your triggers, your habits, and your priorities— *before* you plunge into the numbers and payoff strategy stuff.

Unlike weight, which is on the outside, debt is an entirely private thing. For better or for worse, people don't walk around with their financial statements flying open. You could be in a room with a hundred people and not be able to tell who has debt and who doesn't (and if you're me, you play this little game a bit more often than you should admit!). Taking control of your debt presents unique internal challenges and *no* external motivation. We need to look inside to tackle those challenges or the outside part isn't going to work.

You may be tempted to skip this part, or to rush through in order to get to the putting-together-a-plan part. Please, I beg you, for the love of all that is lovely: don't. Surging forward into the outer, numbers game without having first turned your gaze inward will make everything so much harder for you. There are exceptions to every rule, of course, but I've seen plans work and not work, and when they don't it is usually because the person didn't look within first.

Everyone wants rules of thumb—and there *are* rules of thumb—but they don't all apply to you. Sorting through them requires a relatively intense level of exploration. Deciding what your priorities are and then figuring out how money can make them happen ("I want to do that, so how can I afford it?"), rather than letting the numbers dictate your priorities

("I can't do that because I can't afford it"), sets you up for lasting change. If you're in this to win this, to truly *dominate* your debt and not just to handle it, do a trust dive and spend some time swimming in this pool of introspection. It will ground you, get you focused, and give all the hard work a foundation and a purpose. (Plus, it's relatively fun!)

Step Three: Organize. After you've gotten to know your debt, your goals, and yourself, it's time to get into the numbers. We'll begin by laying out all the pieces of your financial puzzle and creating an overview of what's going on with you and your money. This part will give you the information you need to map out the terrain before you plan your route.

Step Four: Analyze. When all the data is gathered together and laid out in front of you, it's time to really get into it and figure out what's going on. You know that manic television character who covers a wall in newspaper clippings and pictures, puts pushpins and string between them, and scribbles notes all over them in fierce red marker? This part is like that, but different. As you find answers to questions you didn't even know you had about your money and your financial habits, you will either love this part or you will find it gross and tedious. You may get stuck and want to give up, particularly if you identify as "not a numbers person." I know we're still a few chapters away, but if that happens, remember: your job is just to trust the process. Breathe and keep going. All is well, and it will turn out better than you think.

Step Five: Plan. This is when you take everything you've done so far—learning about your debt, thoroughly exploring yourself, organizing elements of your financial life, and analyzing how you've handled money up to this point—and put it all together into one cohesive strategy to knock out your debt.

Step Six: Implement. To make your plan work, you actually need to work it. I won't sugarcoat this for you: even with a strategy in place, this part is a challenge. You will be breaking habits that aren't serving you and forming new ones that do. Your determination to make your debt a priority may require you to make choices you've never made before and stand up to pressure from both other people and yourself. Stay the course. As you stare your debt straight in the eye, whatever you're feeling now cannot compare to the lightness of being debt-free.

Workouts: Each chapter includes information, examples, a framework, and workouts that, if you complete them, will actually *be* your debt-dominating plan.

I call these workouts for a couple of reasons. One is about me: the original incarnation of my business was "financial fitness" and it's the last vestige of that little piece of history. The other is about you! We "exercise" for the sake of it, but we work out in pursuit of a goal. In this book, we don't exercise. We work out. We strive to complete goals. We solve problems. We make sh*t happen.

In this book we will be creating your strategy to *pay off* your debt. We will not be dealing with bankruptcy, debt collectors, or settlements. Also, while this book will help you understand and deal with mortgages and car loans, our primary focus is helping you tackle student loans and/or credit card debt.

There are lessons in here, and questions for you to answer, and space for you to actually work and play. By the end, the work you have done will become your playbook. You will have everything you need to take control, owe less, and live more (read: get out of debt, stay out, and feel amazing).

Plus, as of the publication date, templates, workouts, and plenty of other goodies are also available online! So if you prefer to rock things digitally, look out for links to snag the bonus resources associated with this book and we can hang out on the interwebs at **OweLessLiveMore.com.**

Let's Rock This!

If you need to read things through a few times before you actually do the workouts, or if you prefer to skim then come back to the book in a few months or even a few years… that's all fine. Just be sure to *do it.* It's not all hard, and it's not all boring, but it is going to require you to make it a priority. Reading this book all the way through will not be enough. Like riding a bike or driving a car, if you're serious about paying off your debt, you've got to get out on the road.

If you purchased this copy of the book, you can write on the pages. Get messy! Make it your own! This is a workbook *and* a playbook, after all—you've got the space to create your personal debt domination strategy right here, right now. Own the way you work best, whichever way that is, and keep moving forward.

A note about taking it a step further: I haven't held anything back here, so if you're a self-starter and motivated, you'll find everything you need in these pages. But if, in reading this, you realize you're digging my vibe and you'd like a little bit more personal attention or a kick in the skinny jeans from me, you can get that, too. I'm a real person, I teach debt domination and coach people through it for a living, and you can absolutely work with me one on one and/or hang out with me and other kickass ladies like yourself in one of my Boot Camps. Learn more about these options at **OweLessLiveMore.com.**

Throughout this process, having the right support is *everything*. This means getting clear on what you want and asking for what you need—financially and emotionally—in order to go for it. Find someone you trust, who understands, and who is invested in your outcome, to cheer you on.

Does this feel like a lot? It is. But I've got you. The only things that are important right now are that you trust that being in control is a process, and that living a life without debt is not only entirely possible, it's *going to happen for you.*

So. Grab onto my hand, hold tight, and let's rock this.

The Pledge

Your first action step is a commitment!

I hereby pledge to:

- Embrace my thoughts and my plans; I will not self-edit.
- Be kind to myself; I will not judge or beat myself up for what's already done.
- Stay focused and consistent; I will not hide from or avoid the aspects of my financial situation that make me uncomfortable.
- Seek support when I need it; I will honor what I need and ask questions when I don't understand.

By the end of this chapter you will...

- Understand what debt is.
- Understand how your debt works to keep you in debt and what you can do about it.

Step One: *educate*

What is Debt?

Let's start with what debt is.

Debt is created when you borrow money to buy or pay for something *now* and agree to pay it back at some point *later.* In exchange for having this money *now*, you pay a fee to the person who or institution that loaned it to you, calculated as a percentage of the amount given. That "thank you for letting me have this money" fee is called **interest**.

How thankful do you have to be? That's up to the lender. You can ask them to work with you, but ultimately it's their call. Which means sometimes the fee you pay as a "thank you" far exceeds the level of gratitude you feel about what you used the money for in the first place.

The amount you originally borrowed is called the **principal**. (Not "principle." Like the person in charge of your high school, the amount you originally borrowed is your PAL!) Your principal needs to be given love and attention in the form of cashmoney. Your lender will always apply payments to interest and fees first, then to principal. So your payments must always be large enough to cover all three of those things in order for you to actually be paying off your debt.

"Good" and "Bad" Debt

There are six major types of debt:

1. Student loans
2. Credit card ("consumer") debt
3. Mortgage loans
4. Car loans
5. Bank loans (personal or business)
6. Arrears or bills in collections

The terms "good debt" and "bad debt" are bandied about, and everyone has their own take on them, so here's mine. When you get right down to it, the difference between "good" and "bad" debt has more to do with the lender than with you. Debt is considered "good" when the lender has made a safe bet; i.e., there's a pretty good chance the debt will be repaid. "Good debt" is **secured** or **guaranteed** by something or someone.

Mortgages and car loans are considered "good debt" because they are secured by the house or the car they helped to purchase. If you don't make your mortgage or car payments, your bank can take your house or car from you. (Obviously there are a lot of steps to go through first, but this is possible.)

Federal student loans are also generally considered to be "good debt" because although they are not secured by anything—congrats! your degree is yours for life—they are guaranteed by the government. This means that if you **default**, or don't make all your payments, your lender can still get its money from the government.

Because "good debt" involves less risk to the lender, it tends to come with a few perks for you. For example, you may be able to deduct the interest paid on mortgages and student loans from your taxes. If you qualify for this benefit, you won't pay taxes on the portion of your income that was used to pay the interest. You also have more refinancing options and payment plans if you can't pay.

Here are some other reasons to categorize debt as "good":

- Borrowing money to purchase your home can be a good investment if you can sell the house for profit, and/or you eventually have no home payments.
- Borrowing money to purchase your car saves you money if you can sell the car and get some money back, and/or you eventually have no car payments.
- Borrowing money to invest in your education increases your earning potential, leading to more and better job opportunities.

"Bad debt," on the other hand, has high interest rates, is unsecured, provides no tax breaks, and includes no built-in repayment options that make it easier to lower, postpone, or end payments. "Bad debt" may adversely affect your credit report or credit score. And "bad debt" has a negative emotional charge; debt is "bad" when it makes you feel bad!

So let's be real. Good or bad, *all* debt costs you time, money, and freedom. Sometimes the tradeoff will be worth it (and you won't feel bad), and sometimes it isn't (and you will). Debt is what debt does. It's not "good." It's not "bad." It's just debt.

Feeding the Beast: Interest

So back to interest.

Your debt is a parasitic, money-sucking monster. It needs interest to live; interest is its lifeblood. As you start to kill it off, your debt stays alive because of the interest it consumes every month. Om nom nom.

The secret to killing off your debt is understanding when and how much it eats—how interest is calculated.

For both student loans and credit card debt, although you only have to make one payment per month, you are actually being charged interest every single day. This daily interest is charged in one of two ways: it either **compounds** or it **accrues**.

Credit card interest compounds daily. This means that interest is being charged on the original amount *and* on the interest. So the amount you owe increases daily, and the interest charged today gets added to your principal balance. Tomorrow you are charged interest on the principal and the interest. The next day you will be charged interest on the principal and the interest on the interest and so on, until you make your next payment.

Student loan interest accrues daily. Accruing interest means that the interest is being charged on the principal each day, but not on the interest. The amount you owe still goes up each day just not quite as much, because while you are charged interest on the principal, you are not charged interest on the interest.

How Interest Really Works: APR + Compounding Interest

You are probably familiar with your credit card interest rate, but that interest rate doesn't give you the full story. Let's say your interest rate is 18%. The full story is contained in the three little letters after the % sign that probably never meant anything to you before but will now: APR.

APR stands for **Annual Percentage Rate**. What that means is "an interest rate that averages out to be approximately 18% each year."

Here's where it gets crazy. Your credit card company tells you that you're being charged an annual rate of 18%, but that's not what it's actually charging you. Remember, when the interest is charged it either compounds or accrues *every day*.

The credit card company gives you the APR to keep things nice and simple, but what they are actually using to calculate your interest is something called a **Daily Periodic Rate**, or DPR. The DPR is the APR divided by the number of days in the year, or 365. To sum this up:

- You are charged interest each day based on a daily rate.
- You pay all the interest you are charged once a month.
- Your interest rate is displayed as an annual rate.

So what 18% APR really means is that your debt monster is gobbling up your money at a rate of 18% divided by 365, or 0.0493%, each and every day.

Math Time! How Compounding Interest is Calculated

Now, let's use some real numbers to really hit this home.

Example:

For an APR of 18%, the actual daily interest rate is 18% / 365 or 0.0493%. This percentage can also be written as 0.000493. Here's how compounding interest would affect a balance of $10,000:

Day 1 - $10,000.00

* Interest charged: $10,000.00 x 0.000493 = $4.93
* New amount owed: $10,000.00 + $4.93 = **$10,004.93**

Day 2 - $10,004.93

* Interest charged: $10,004.93 x 0.000493 = $4.93
* New amount owed: $10,004.93 + $4.93 = **$10,009.86**

Day 3 - $10,009.86

* Interest charged: $10,009.86 x 0.000493 = $4.93
* New amount owed: $10,009.86 + $4.93 = **$10,014.79**

Day 4 - $10,014.79

* Interest charged: $10,014.79 x 0.000493 = $4.94
* New amount owed: $10,014.79 + $4.94 = **$10,019.73**

Day 5 - $10,019.73

* Interest charged: $10,019.73 x 0.000493 = $4.94
* New amount owed: $10,019.73 + $4.94 = **$10,024.67**

By Day 30, your $10,000 balance will have racked up $149.01 in interest. If you make a $75.00 payment, you will not see the balance go down.

Confusing? Yes, at first. Most people just pay and shut up without trying to understand it. Your credit card company doesn't really care if you know this. Even if someone bothers to explain this to you, he or she may go on to say, "don't worry about memorizing this information." (I didn't make that up. That is actual language from an actual credit card company's website.)

I disagree. You should be *very* worried about memorizing this information because if you are carrying a balance, your credit card company (or student loan company, for that matter) *is taking a lot of your money* based on this information. Lending companies bank (literally!) on your not caring about this. And they will continue to do so until the end of time or until your debt is paid off, whichever happens sooner.

Yes, it sucks. This part isn't designed to make you feel better. It's designed to be a wakeup call, to get you sitting up a little straighter, and to get the wheels turning. I'm guessing you already knew your debt was costing you money. Now you know how much. Later on, when we get to your get-out-and-stay-out strategy, this perspective will give you the ability to make decisions based on emotions, goals, *and* cold hard cash.

Compound Interest: Good or Evil?

Compound interest definitely works against you when it comes to money you borrow, but it actually works for you when it comes to money you hold and grow. When you've saved or invested the money, you earn the compound interest rather than pay it. Same equation, opposite direction in your bank account. That's how people with a lot of investments are able to live off of them—the money generates money and it's paid out on a regular basis, such as monthly or quarterly. Knock out your debt and this will be you! So much better to grow and hold than borrow, right?

How Interest Really Works: APR and Accruing Interest

Federal student loans use a model called **simplified daily interest**. In this model, interest does not compound (so you don't pay interest on the interest each day), but it does accrue (meaning until you make a payment, you always owe more today than you did yesterday). The amount you are charged will be similar to but a little less than what you would be charged if the interest were compounding.

As with your credit card company, your federal student loan company will give you a nice, neat, simple interest rate, set by Congress, that doesn't tell the whole story. Federal student loan interest is calculated using something called the "**interest rate factor**" which, similar to the credit card DPR, is your interest rate divided by the number of days in the year. The amount of interest charged each day is your Principal Balance x Number of Days Since Your Last Payment x Interest Rate Factor.

How Interest Really Works: Amortization

A mortgage is a fancy way of saying "loan secured by real property" or, in other words, "loan based on our ability to take your house away from you if you don't pay."

A mortgage is likely the most amount of debt you will ever carry. If you don't have a mortgage, it's better to understand it now so you don't get in over your head later. Since we're out for total debt domination, here's how mortgages work.

Mortgages, car loans, and other types of amortized loans are repaid based on an amortization schedule. **Amortization** is a very fancy word that basically means, "We've figured out how much interest you're going to pay and we've spread it out over the entire term of the loan, *but* we're going to ensure you pay most of it early on in the term so even if you pay off the loan early we've still squeezed as much money as possible out of you. Wahoo!"

Mortgages and car loans generally work the same way. You pay one fixed, monthly amount. For the first half of your loan term, you pay mostly interest. Halfway through the term, you switch over to paying more and more principal until the loan is paid off.

To figure out how much the "thank you" fee on your mortgage costs you each month, you'll need to know four things about your mortgage:

1. Term
2. Principal
3. Interest rate (annual and monthly)
4. Monthly payment

More math and more real numbers coming your way to illustrate this...

Example:

Let's say these are the details of your mortgage:

1. **Term:** 30 years
2. **Principal:** $100,000
3. **Interest rate:** 6% annually and 6% / 12 = 0.5% (which can also be written 0.005) monthly
4. **Monthly payment:** $600

Here's how amortization plays out!

Month 1 - Interest is charged on a principal balance of $100,000.00, which means that of your $600 monthly payment you pay...

* $500.00 in interest ($100,000.00 x 0.005)
* $100.00 toward principal ($600.00 - $500.00)

After your payment, your remaining principal balance is $100,000.00 - $100.00 = **$99,900.00.**

Month 2 - Interest is charged on a principal balance of $99,900.00, which means that of your $600 monthly payment you pay...

* $499.50 in interest ($99,900.00 x 0.005)
* $100.50 toward principal ($600.00 - $499.50) (50 cents more than last month—yay!)

Your remaining principal balance is $99,900.00 - $100.50 = **$99,799.50.**

Month 3 - You pay...

* $499.00 in interest ($99,799.50 x 0.005, rounded up)
* $101.00 toward principal ($600.00 - $499.00)

Your remaining principal balance is $99,799.50 - $101.00 = **$99,698.50.**

Month 4 - You pay...

* $498.49 in interest ($99,698.50 x 0.005)
* $101.51 toward principal ($600.00 - $498.49)

Your remaining principal balance is $99,698.50 - $101.51 = **$99,596.99.**

And so on for thirty years, or 30 x 12 = 360 payments.

Here is a handy chart to summarize the differences between the types of debt discussed in this chapter:

TYPE OF DEBT	YOUR PAYMENT EACH MONTH	HOW INTEREST IS CHARGED	HOW INTEREST IS CALCULATED EACH MONTH
Credit cards	Minimum payment based on credit card company's calculations	Daily compounding interest	Daily Percentage Rate (DPR): APR divided by 365
Federal student loans	Minimum payment based on payment plan	Simplified daily interest	"Interest Rate Factor": interest rate divided by 365
Mortgages and car loans	Minimum payment based on payment plan	Monthly amortized interest	APR divided by 12

Other Important Things to Know About Interest

There are three types of interest rates: (1) ones that can change, (2) ones that can't, and (3) ones that will change after a pre-determined period of time.

(1) Fixed interest rates stay the same for the lifetime of the debt. Mortgages, federal student loans, car loans, and many personal or bank loans come in fixed-interest varieties, but not all do, so pay close attention to this.

(2) Variable interest rates can fluctuate over the lifetime of the debt at the whim of your lender, credit card company, or the federal government. Nearly all credit cards have variable interest rates. There is a cap on how high the interest can go, but that cap is often way higher than anything you'd want to pay. Be aware that your credit card company may charge a different interest rate for purchases than for balance transfers or cash advances, and if you have transferred a balance, the interest rate for new purchases may be different from the interest rate attached to the transferred balance.

(3) Promotional interest rates are lower rates that are locked in for a pre-established period of time and then go up at the expiration of that period. At that point they will switch over to either a fixed or variable rate. Many credit card companies will give you promotional rates to entice you to open or switch cards. Be very, very careful! The interest rate may start out delightfully low… but then it will go up like whoa. Additionally, student loan companies sometimes offer promotional interest rates if you opt for a service they provide, such as paperless statements, automatic payments, or on-time payments. These benefits will lower your payment by a fraction of a percent, and although that seems like a small amount, it can mean you will pay thousands of dollars less over the lifetime of the loan.

One more thing to be aware of is **capitalized interest**, which is a horrible (yet totally real) thing that happens when your lender doesn't require you to make payments but still charges you interest. When your loans enter repayment, the lender takes all the interest that has been piling up, plops it on top of your principal, and starts charging you interest on that new amount. If your student loans are deferred because you're still in school, unemployed, or experiencing financial hardship, just be aware that the interest meter may still be clicking merrily along.

So. Now you know. And knowing's half the battle. The other half is what we're going to do in the rest of this book.

Step One Workouts: Educate

I commit to doing these workouts on [date(s)]: ____________________

Workout #1.1: Preliminary Debt Information

1. These are the kinds of debt I have:

   -
   -
   -
   -
   -
   -

2. These debts have fixed interest:

   -
   -
   -
   -
   -
   -

3. These debts have capitalized interest rates:

* *
* *
* *
* *
* *
* *

4. The interest on these debts is compounding:

* *
* *
* *
* *
* *
* *

5. The interest on these debts is accruing:

* *
* *
* *

6. The interest on these debts is amortized:

* *
* *
* *

Workout #1.2: Emotional Check-In

Because being on top of money is about what you do and how you feel, check in with yourself here. Remember this is an inside-out and outside-in process!

- Before this chapter I…

- Now I…

- The most helpful / effective portion of this chapter for me was…

- The least helpful / effective portion of this chapter for me was…

* I was really surprised that / by...

* The three questions this chapter raised for me are…

* My #1 takeaway from this chapter is…

* I also want to note that…

For support and bonus resources to accompany these workouts, come hang out at **OweLessLiveMore.com**!

By the end of this chapter you will...

- Clarify what you want and why you want it.
- Bless and release anything that is in your way.

Step Two: *set goals*

We just spent some time getting to know your debt; now we are going to spend some time getting to know *you*. Creating a plan to dominate your debt means uncovering the answers to three questions:

1. Where do I want to go?
2. Where am I now?
3. How am I going to get to where I want to go?

Taking control of your debt is really about choices. The more you understand about your choices and how you make them, the more closely aligned they will be to what you truly want. Understanding yourself is the key to making the choices that will lead you to freedom from debt.

We start with Point B (where you want to go) rather than Point A (where you are now). Don't get me wrong, we're going to spend plenty of time analyzing where you are now, because that will give us a lot of insight into your patterns and habits and ensure you create a plan that is realistic and doable. But we're not going to start there.

When you start with goals, not numbers, your focus is squarely on what is actually important to you. That's going to be a lot more motivating than a bunch of digits and decimal points. In other words, taking control of your debt is far easier when you have a reason for getting out of debt other than "I don't want to have debt anymore because debt sucks."

Don't skip this step. These workouts may seem mushy and abstract, especially if you're more of a lines-and-grids type of girl, but they are the foundation for everything. When you know your *why*, your *what* will fall into place much more easily. Plus, the clearer you are about where you want to go, the more brightly illuminated the path (and the hotter the fire under your bum) to get there.

So if you're planning to read through the whole book, come back and do the workouts in this chapter. Spend some serious time on them. My clients and my Dominate Your Debt™ Boot Campers spend a solid week or even two weeks on this step. Don't worry if you aren't sure what to say. Just give it a go. You can always come back and re-evaluate as your life shifts and changes.

Most importantly, make sure you're both reading *and* writing. Writing makes it real.

Step Two Workouts: Set Goals

I commit to doing these workouts on [date(s)]: ______________________________

Workout #2.1: Wear Your Sunglasses at Night

It is vitally important that you have a "So I can..." for your debt.

Career fulfillment was my biggest "So I can...". I wanted to be free from *needing* to work at a large corporate law firm in order to make the minimum payment on my debt. What is yours?

I want to pay off my debt so I can...

Goal #1:

Goal #2:

Goal #3:

If you catch yourself writing down any goals that have to do with money, push yourself further. Keep asking "so I can…" until you arrive at something that feels really juicy, expansive, and awesome.

Here are some prompts to help you identify these:

* My secret dream is…

* Having debt would stop me or slow me down because…

* Five to ten years ago, I…

* Five to ten years from now I want…

Workout #2.2: Doing / Being / Having / Feeling

Now that you're a little clearer about your "So I can..." let's break it down even further into what your life as a debt dominatrix will look like. Those items fall into four categories: (1) what you can *do*, (2) who you can *be*, (3) what you can *have*, and (4) how you can *feel*. So let's play. Light a candle, crank some tunes, take a deep breath, and answer these questions. Focus and don't edit yourself.

DOING: When my debt is paid off I will be able to do…

- That is different from now in that…

- This is important to me because…

BEING: When my debt is paid off I will be able to be…

* That is different from now in that…

* This is important to me because…

HAVING: When my debt is paid off I will be able to have…

* This is different from now in that…

* This is important to me because…

FEELING: When my debt is paid off I will feel…

- That is different from now in that…

- This is important to me because…

Other thoughts I have are. . .

Workout #2.3: Bless + Release

Now that you've envisioned life without debt, it's time to bless and release it. Again, no self-editing. It's okay that you have this debt right now. It's time to understand it, thank it, and then let it go.

- My debt was created when…

- I am in debt because…

- With the money I borrowed, I paid for…

- I borrowed the money for this (rather than pay for it outright) because…

* As a result of being in debt, I was able to do / be / have...

* The best thing about my debt is...

* The worst thing about my debt is...

* My biggest regret about my debt is...

- I don't at all regret…

- If I didn't have debt, I would not have had access to…

- Another option for me was…

- I didn't choose that because…

* If I hadn't had debt, my life would be...

* If I hadn't had the option to go into debt, I would have...

* If I hadn't had the option to go into debt, I could have...

* I choose differently now because...

Workout #2.4: Drowning Out the Noise

Taking control of your debt may mean uprooting some deeply-rooted ideas about money. Your current relationship with money now will help you determine how to change it.

- What are some of the things you have heard about debt?

- What parts do you know to be true?

- Why?

* What parts are you not sure about?

* Why?

* What would it take to be sure about those things?

* What parts do you know are not true?

* How do you know?

Now we're going to really drown out the noise! Create playlists that will be the soundtrack to your debt domination journey. Try a mellow one, a pumped-up one, a throwback one, or even a cheesy girl power one.

My Playlists + Top Debt-Dominating Songs

By the end of this chapter you will...

* Have a list of all your debts.
* Know how much money you have coming in and going out each month.
* Have a complete overview of your spending.
* Understand your repayment options.

Step Three: *organize*

Yes, getting organized takes up an entire chapter! If Point B represents the goals you identified in the last chapter, this chapter is about Point A—figuring out where you are so you can create the path you'll follow to get from A to B.

Organizing your finances sets up your workspace. You don't have to think too much during this part, so it will help to clear your mind, which will make things much more efficient later. That way, when you really get down to business and it's time to think and make choices, you won't get bogged down looking for things or having to remember them. Everything you need will be right there in front of you.

As far as *what* to organize, there's bad news and good news. The bad news is, taking control of your debt really requires you to be on top of everything related to your finances. Debt is only one piece of the puzzle. The key to a successful debt-dominating plan is to fit all the pieces together and then find balance, balance, and more balance.

The good news is, this isn't a five-thousand-piece jigsaw with no edges. There are only five pieces to your financial puzzle, and everyone's are the same: Bills, Budget, Debt, Savings, and Investments. Together, we will affectionately refer to them as your "bee-bee-dees plus eye" (BBDS+I). We'll go over what "organizing" means for each of your BBDS+I, and then it's workout time!

Bills

Your bills are the recurring expenses for which you are responsible each month, whether you pay them automatically or not. Your bills will have the greatest impact on your ability to dominate your debt. Organizing your bills means creating a list of exactly what you have committed to pay each month before the month even starts.

Budget

Your bills give you a clear picture of what you *will* spend. Your budget is a plan for what you *should* spend. Organizing your spending prepares you for a successful budget by looking at what you *do* spend. A budget is a magical tool that will help you take control of your debt, and we're going to spend a lot of time creating one that feels real and authentically yours. We're going to dig deep into your spending—possibly deeper than you have ever gone before—because your budget is far more likely to work for you when you have a solid grasp of both *how* you spend and *why*.

Debt

Kind of why we're here, right? Organizing your debt means having one grand master list of every single one of your debts including all the hot and spicy details about each debt.

Savings

There is one universal truth to remember about savings, and that is your ABCs:

> **A**lways
>
> **B**e
>
> **C**-ing money in your savings account

Organizing your savings means taking stock of what is already in your accounts and getting clear on the role you want savings to play in your life. Balancing debt and savings is like the three bears! You don't want to save too much and you don't want to save too little. You have to get it just right.

+ Investments

Organizing your investments means having one grand master list of all your invested assets and the details of each. However! There's a little "+" before the "I" in BBDS+I because investments are a bonus. Yes, you need them; investments are the golden ticket to financial freedom. No, you are not a terrible, horrible, no good, very bad person if you don't have them yet. Keep investments in the back of your mind while you're tackling your debt. If you're stressed about not having (or even understanding) investments, you have my permission to relax. We'll get there.

The reason to have investments is so you don't work until the end of time. If you invest well, your money will grow and generate income to support you when you can no longer rely on a paycheck for your income. It is tricky to invest while you're paying off debt, but at the very least you can contribute to a 401(k) or an IRA. You will be happy you did. Even if it's just a little bit, that money will grow and grow, and—through the magic of compound interest—you will be so happy you started now. I know it's hard. But if you wait ten more years to begin saving for retirement, you will be ten years behind. If at all humanly possible, you want to be starting something *now*.

This organizational step is all about making sure you have an easy, systematic way of tracking each of these BBDS+I areas to ensure nothing falls through the cracks. So let's get rocking.

Step Three Workouts: Organize

I commit to doing these workouts on [date(s)]: ______________________________

Note: You can do all these workouts in one day, or over the course of several weeks. Whatever you choose is totally fine. And remember, we're just getting organized now. Stick to the workouts; there's no need to do anything with this information just yet.

Workout #3.1: Debt Overview

Step One: Gather all the information for each of your debts. This includes statements, phone numbers, and usernames and password hints. We will use this information to create an overview of your debt.

I don't have many hard and fast rules about finance, but this is one: you *must* have all your debt laid out in one place. This prevents you from thinking about this credit card or that credit card, or that some kinds of debt are good debt and some are bad. Use this checklist to make sure no debt slips through the cracks.

Gather Your Debt: The Checklist

Credit Cards

- ☐ Major credit cards
- ☐ Store credit cards

Student Loans

- ☐ Federal loans
- ☐ Private loans
- ☐ Consolidation loans

Secured Loans

- ☐ Mortgage
- ☐ Car loan

Miscellaneous Debt

- ☐ Personal bank loan
- ☐ Bank overdraft loan
- ☐ Medical bills
- ☐ Borrowed from friends/family
- ☐ Other:

Chart Your Debt: The Details

Step Two: Enter the information about your debt into the chart on the next two pages. Here are the essential details to know:

* **Lender Name (Type)**: AmEx (Credit Card), SallieMae (Student Loan), etc.
* **Due Day**: The day of the month your payment is due (4, 19, etc.).
* **Minimum Payment**: The minimum amount your lender requires you to pay each month.
* **Principal Balance**: The total amount of remaining principal.
* **Interest Rate**: The % interest you are charged each year (APR).
* **Fixed / Variable**: Whether the interest rate is fixed or variable.
* **Payoff Amount**: If you continue making the minimum payment, the amount you will have paid, including interest, when the debt is completely repaid. This information may be difficult to find, but it is available to you.
* **Original Loan Amount**: The amount you originally borrowed for secured debt and student loans.
* **Payoff Date (far in the future)**: The date by which, if you make the minimum payment each month, the loan will be completely paid off.
* **Origination Date**: The date you first incurred the debt (for credit cards, the oldest transaction you can find that you haven't yet paid off completely).

You can gather this information in one big block of time or over a few days or even a few weeks. Some of these items may be harder to find than others, and you may need to call your lender and ask them some questions. Have a glass of your favorite beverage, listen to one of the playlists you created in Workout #2.4, and decide what fabulous reward to offer yourself when you're done!

Debt Overview

LENDER NAME (TYPE)	DUE DAY	MINIMUM PAYMENT	PRINCIPAL BALANCE	INTEREST RATE

FIXED OR VARIABLE?	PAYOFF AMOUNT	ORIGINAL LOAN AMOUNT	PAYOFF DATE (FAR IN THE FUTURE)	ORIGINATION DATE

Workout #3.2: Your Bills

Now that you've gathered all your debt and laid it out in one place, it's time to do the same with your bills.

Gather all the information for each of your bills this month. This includes statements, phone numbers, and usernames and password hints. No estimates or averages here! Find the physical bill or log in to your account and get the exact amount. Use this checklist to make sure no bills slip through the cracks:

Gather Your Bills: The Checklist

Income

- [ ] Paycheck
- [ ] Other income

Memberships and Subscriptions

- [ ] Gym
- [ ] Video streaming
- [ ] Music streaming

Debt

- [ ] Major credit cards
- [ ] Store credit cards
- [ ] Student loans

Utilities and Living Expenses

- [ ] Electric and gas
- [ ] Cable
- [ ] Cell phone
- [ ] Insurance
- [ ] Car payment
- [ ] Water bill
- [ ] HOA or condo fees

Other

- [ ]
- [ ]
- [ ]
- [ ]

At the core, you need to know only two basic things about your money: what comes in, and how much goes out. The mistake most people make is that they figure this out reactively. You must determine this every month *before the month starts*. Once you know what you've already committed to spending, you can decide what to do with what's left.

Enter this month's bills into the chart on the next page. For subsequent months, set up a new chart or spreadsheet on your own.

(Remember, there isn't much thinking that goes along with this. We're not creating a plan here; we're just getting organized. Plug the numbers in and go. We'll get to the planning and analysis later.)

The chart has six columns:

1. **Day Due**: The date the bill is due (not the day that you pay it!).
2. **Bill Name**: The name of the bill payee.
3. **Amount Out**: All the bills you're committed to paying this month.
4. **Amount In**: All of your take-home pay.
5. **Total**: The total Amount In minus the total Amount Out. This is what you have left for savings, paying off debt, and all the things you will buy this month.
6. **Notes**: Anything else you'd like to remember.

Here's an example of what it might look like when you're done:

DAY DUE	BILL NAME	AMOUNT OUT	AMOUNT IN	TOTAL (IN - OUT)	NOTES
1	Rent	$1,200.00			
4	Paycheck 1		$2,000.00		
5	Student loan	$800.00			
6	Cell phone	$100.00			
12	Electric	$75.00			
14	Credit Card 1	$100.00			
15	Gym	$100.00			
18	Paycheck 2		$2,000.00		
20	Credit Card 2	$75.00			
23	Cable	$150.00			
	Total	$2,600.00	$4,000.00	**$1,400.00**	

My Bills for the Month of: ___________________________

DAY DUE	BILL NAME	AMOUNT OUT	AMOUNT IN	TOTAL (IN - OUT)	NOTES
	Total				

Workout #3.3: Spending Round-Up

In order to figure out what you *should* spend to hit your goals, first we need to know what you *do* spend. And we're going to figure that out manually. Line by line. Old school style.

In this workout, you will:

1 Gather all the details of your spending for the past three months.

2. List them in the Spending Round-Up chart in this workout.

3. Choose eight to twelve categories that will capture each of the items.

4. Assign a category to each transaction.

Be sure these categories are narrow enough to reflect your lifestyle (one of my clients had a category for wine!) but not so narrow that you have twenty-five of them. Also, wherever possible, avoid the "Miscellaneous" category. No financial junk drawers here! Try to figure out what's in that category and put it where it belongs. Check out the categories in the example for inspiration.

Yes, there are shiny apps that will pull all the information from each of your accounts, categorize it, and run a report for you. But that's not the point of this workout. This is not just about writing in numbers, it's about internalizing them.

To make this task slightly less onerous: Most banks and credit card companies allow you to download a list of all of your activity, dating back at least three months, in a variety of formats. If you are comfortable with spreadsheets, I can't recommend this highly enough as it eliminates the need to write or type out each individual transaction and makes it easier to assign categories and sort the data to complete this workout.

1. Log in to your account and look for a link that says "Download Activity."

2. You will see a number of formatting options. Select Comma Separated Values or .csv (this is the spreadsheet equivalent of a plain text file).

3. Once downloaded, open the file with any spreadsheet program.

4. Copy and paste the activity into one master spreadsheet, create a "Category" column, assign a category to each transaction, and you are good to go.

This may sound tedious, but I promise that once you get into it, it won't be as bad or take as long as you think it will. (Now's a great time for that pumped-up playlist!)

Here's an example of what it might look like when you're done:

PURCHASE DATE	DESCRIPTION	AMOUNT	CATEGORY
1	ABC Grocery	$40.00	Groceries
1	Bullseye	$100.00	Household
5	Yummy Sandwiches	$10.00	Food - Fast Food
6	Yummy Sandwiches	$10.00	Food - Fast Food
9	Yummy Sandwiches	$12.00	Food - Fast Food
10	Delicious Lattes	$5.00	Food - Fast Food
11	Candelight Lounge	$60.00	Food - Restaurant
12	Delicious Lattes	$4.00	Food - Fast Food
14	Scrumptious Soaps	$25.00	Gifts
15	Bangin' Concert	$100.00	Entertainment
16	ABC Grocery	$45.00	Groceries
16	Yummy Sandwiches	$8.00	Food - Fast Food
17	Blamazon	$15.00	Entertainment
18	Bullseye	$100.00	Household
18	Yummy Sandwiches	$10.00	Food - Fast Food
19	Chandelier Lounge	$80.00	Food - Restaurant
19	Taxi	$20.00	Transportation
20	Eggs n Benedict	$40.00	Food - Restaurant
21	Yummy Sandwiches	$12.00	Food - Fast Food
21	ABC Grocery	$70.00	Groceries
22	Hot Lattes	$8.00	Food - Fast Food
23	Blamazon	$100.00	Household

PURCHASE DATE	DESCRIPTION	AMOUNT	CATEGORY
24	Yummy Sandwiches	$10.00	Food - Fast Food
25	Doctor Doctor	$20.00	Co-Pay
26	Yummy Sandwiches	$12.00	Food - Fast Food
27	Hot Lattes	$8.00	Food - Fast Food
28	Yummy Sandwiches	$20.00	Food - Fast Food
28	Eggs n Benedict	$40.00	Food - Restaurant
29	Shiny Nails	$40.00	Health + Beauty
30	Marvelous Makeup	$50.00	Health + Beauty

Pep Talk: We are not trying to get insight into how much you suck with money—there really isn't any such thing as that—so if this workout makes you feel sh*tty (totally normal!), go ahead and feel sh*tty, but put a time limit on it. We need to see where your money has been going. It doesn't matter if it's out of the ordinary or split among three methods of payment. We need to know everything, and it needs to be clearly laid out so your plan is grounded in what's real for you now.

Spending Round-Up

PURCHASE DATE	DESCRIPTION	AMOUNT	CATEGORY

PURCHASE DATE	DESCRIPTION	AMOUNT	CATEGORY

Spending Round-Up, Continued

PURCHASE DATE	DESCRIPTION	AMOUNT	CATEGORY

Workout #3.4: Savings

Let's get you clear on the relationship you have and would like to have with savings.

Truth time!

- The total in my savings account(s) right now is: $______________.
- I would like to have this amount: $______________.
- The reason I would like to have that amount is...

Multiple Choice! 

My current relationship with my savings account looks like this…

- ☐ I regularly add money to a savings account and leave it there.
- ☐ I regularly add money to a savings account and take it out again.
- ☐ I have a savings account with some money in it, but I don't really put money in or take money out.
- ☐ I have a savings account but there is no money in it.
- ☐ I don't have a savings account.

Digging Deeper...

- The relationship I would like to have with my savings account is...

- When I think about saving, I…

Workout #3.5: Investments

Let's get you clear on the relationship you have and would like to have with investing.

Truth time!

* The total amount I have invested is: $______________.
* I would like to have this amount: $_________________.
* The reason I would like to have that amount is...

Multiple Choice! 

My current relationship with investing looks like this…

- ☐ I regularly add money to an investment or retirement account.
- ☐ I have an investment or retirement account but I'm not adding money to it.
- ☐ I manage my own investment account and/or have an active relationship with a financial planner.
- ☐ Someone else manages my investment account for me.
- ☐ I don't have an investment account.

Digging Deeper...

- The relationship I would like to have with investing is...

- When I think about investing, I…

Workout #3.6: More Money

Brainstorm ways you can bring in more money. While you may never have to do any of these things, this workout is all about empowering you to show that you have options. (Yes, even if they stink, they're still options!) Don't self-edit here.

Workout #3.7: Emotional Check-In

Because being on top of money is about what you do *and* how you feel, let's check in. How do you feel about what you accomplished in this chapter?

* Before this chapter I…

* Now I…

* The most helpful / effective portion of this chapter for me was…

* The least helpful / effective portion of this chapter for me was…

- I was really surprised that / by...

- The three questions this chapter raised for me are…

- My #1 takeaway from this chapter is…

- I also want to note that…

Workout #3.8: Play Date!

Now go do something nice for yourself! A warm bath, a hug, a mani / pedi— something that is going to make you feel *amazing*! You've earned it.

For support and bonus resources to accompany these workouts, come hang out at **OweLessLiveMore.com**!

By the end of this mini-chapter you will...

- Understand the various types of federal student loans and repayment options.
- Be organized and on top of your loans.
- Know what questions to ask to get the information you don't yet have.

Student Loans

Student loans get their own featured mini-chapter because they are truly exceptional in the amount of flexibility you have with paying them off. Second only to a mortgage, student loans are likely the heaviest debt burden you will ever carry, especially if you took out loans for graduate school. If you don't have student loan debt, feel free to skip this chapter (and be happy it doesn't apply to you!).

While student loan repayment options are flexible, you *do* have to pay them off. Student loans are virtually impossible to discharge in bankruptcy. You are on the hook for your student loans unless and until they are forgiven, you pay them off, or you die.

If you have federal student loans, get acquainted with the U.S. Department of Education's Federal Student Aid website, currently located at **studentaid.ed.gov**. I've intentionally kept the information in this chapter as general as possible because the legislation governing student loans is constantly evolving.

Types of Student Loans

Student loans come from two sources: private lenders and the federal government. Among federal loans, there are two kinds of interest: subsidized and unsubsidized. Let's take a peek at all this, shall we?

Private Student Loans

Private student loans are offered by banks, service companies (often the same ones that service federal loans), and any other lender willing to give you money to pay for your education. You can shop around, compare terms and services, and choose the lender that suits you best. The terms of a private loan, particularly if from a reputable bank or company, are likely to be comparable to a business loan—better than a credit card, but not as flexible or attractive as a mortgage. (Remember, private student loan debt is unsecured and therefore the lender faces a greater risk of not being fully repaid.) Because the terms attached to private loans vary so widely, and because none of the myriad benefits that apply to federal loans apply to private loans, the rest of this chapter focuses on federal student loans.

Federal Student Loans

The federal government funds your federal student loans, but as you may have noticed if you have them, you don't deal with the government directly. Instead, you deal with one of the various companies with which the Department of Education contracts to service the loans. Your school may have invited you to choose among several loan servicers at the outset, but beyond that you have no control over the company that services your loans.

This lack of control can be very annoying if you're not happy with elements of the service experience, including customer service, the servicer's website, and even the incentives you are offered. It can also be annoying if you *are* happy with your service and the company sells or transfers your loans to another service company. Unfortunately, you get no say; your only real option is to get rid of the damn loans and be done with the process.

Other than limited choice over the company, federal student loans allow you greater flexibility than any other kind of debt in the plethora of available payment plans, the lower interest rates relative to private loans and credit cards, the ability to postpone payments, and the possibility of complete forgiveness after a period of time.

Subsidized Federal Loans

Subsidized loans are the best kind to have because, provided you meet certain criteria, the federal government *pays the interest for you* in periods of deferment, including while you're in school. If you have subsidized loans and there's any chance you'll be unemployed or facing financial hardship, move them to the bottom of your priority list!

Unsubsidized Federal Loans

As the term suggests, the federal government does *not* pay the interest for you on unsubsidized loans—not now, and not ever. This explains why, if you have them, you owed (or you will owe) a lot more when you graduate(d) than you originally borrowed. All that time you were studying and lounging out in the quad? "*Cha-ching, cha-ching*!" rang the interest cash register on your unsubsidized loans. Unless you pay all that interest within six months of graduation, it gets dumped on top of your loan principal in that sexy move called capitalization.

Federal Repayment Plan Options

There are a variety of repayment plan options available for federal student loans. We'll go over the three that are most popular as of this writing (standard, income-based, and income-based + public interest). To review the additional available repayment plans, visit the Department of Education website at **studentaid.ed.gov**.

Standard

The standard repayment plan is a basic ten-year plan. This is the default plan unless you both qualify and specifically apply for a different one. In the standard plan, the loan company takes the amount you borrowed, tacks on the interest, creates a repayment schedule, and then… *voilà!* You're given a monthly payment that will ensure you've paid off the loan in ten years or 120 payments. Your monthly payment will be the highest under the standard plan, but if you take the full ten years to pay it off, you'll also pay the least amount of interest of any repayment plan.

Income-Based Repayment (IBR)

In Income-Based Repayment, or IBR, your minimum payment is calculated as a percentage of your disposable income. To qualify, the amount of your loans relative to your income must exceed a certain threshold. You must apply for and be granted IBR status every year.

After twenty-five years in the IBR plan (meaning your debt-to-income ratio has been above the qualifying threshold for twenty-five years) any remaining loan balance will be forgiven.

This plan is relatively new, so what will actually happen remains to be seen, but as of this writing, any balance forgiven at the end of the twenty-five years will be taxed as income. For example, if you have $100,000 forgiven, your tax return that year will reflect an additional $100,000 in income, pushing you into a much higher income tax bracket. *Ouch.* It may still be well worth it, particularly if you have so much debt that paying it off really isn't an option, but keep this in mind. And work with a good accountant.

IBR + Public Interest

The Income-Based Repayment + Public Interest plan is similar to the regular IBR plan except your loans will be forgiven in ten years (versus twenty-five) if you work in a field and hold a position the federal government deems to be "public interest." With IBR + Public Interest, you must earn below the income threshold *and* maintain your career in public interest for the entire ten-year duration of this plan.

Extended Repayment

The extended repayment plan is similar to the standard plan, but your payments will be spread over fifteen, twenty, or twenty-five years instead of ten, lowering your monthly payment and increasing the amount of interest you will pay over the lifetime of the loan.

Other Repayment Plans

Additional repayment plans include Graduated, Income-Contingent, Income-Sensitive, and Pay-As-You-Earn. The basic idea of these plans is that, as your income increases over time, so will your minimum payment.

Heads Up! Two Notes about Repayment Plans

Heads-Up Note #1: With most plans tied to your income, your minimum payment will be so low that you won't be keeping ahead of the interest. This means your balance will go up each month even as you're making payments. There may be nothing you can do about this. You may have to wait the ten, fifteen, twenty or twenty-five years to take advantage of loan forgiveness. As painful as the increasing balance may be to watch, keep your eyes on it—it is still your debt and your responsibility.

Heads-Up Note #2: Currently, if you are married and file jointly, your spouse's income but not your spouse's debt is added to your own to determine the income threshold for income-based repayment. A mistake in the rules or the tax code? Who knows. But that's the way it is. If you and your spouse both have student loan debt, and if you intend to apply for any income-based repayment plan, work with an accountant or tax professional who understands the tax repercussions of this type of situation and will ensure your filing status and student loan repayment plan all work out to your greatest benefit.

Consolidation

We're getting a little ahead of ourselves here because this is more of a planning tool than an organizational one, but I include an introduction to consolidation in this chapter because (1) it is a particularly attractive option for federal student loans, and (2) given how often this has come up with my clients, I have a hunch you may already be thinking about it!

Consolidation is so named because it consolidates (combines) a bunch of smaller student loan debts into one larger debt.

The Pros: Consolidation can simplify your payments, lock in your interest rate, and reduce your minimum payment by extending your repayment term.

The Cons: Consolidation makes you think you're saving money, but unless you are locking in a lower interest rate on a variable loan, you actually don't save anything *because you have extended your repayment term*. Your new interest rate is just a weighted average of all your previous interest rates, so no money saved there. Yes, consolidation lowers your minimum payment, but you will be paying it (and all that interest) for longer, and thereby spending much more.

That said, if you ask all the right questions and consolidation is a good option for you, it absolutely can save you money when combined with other strategies. We will revisit this later.

Should You Consolidate? Some questions to ask:

- Do you retain all the benefits of having federal loans?
- Do you retain the incentives of your current loan servicer, and if not, does it still make financial and emotional sense?
- Have you done your research and do you trust the company that would consolidate your loans?
- Are you fully aware of the terms of your new consolidation loan?

If you can answer "yes" to all of these questions, consolidation may be the right move for you.

If You Really Can't Pay: Deferment and Forbearance

If you can't afford the payments under any of the plans due to special circumstances, or if you have a rock 'em sock 'em plan that involves tackling other debts first, you may be able to pause or postpone your payments. As student loan debt climbs higher and higher, fewer and fewer graduates are able to afford their payments, and these options become more and more popular. While they are there to provide you with some relief, just remember that your loans won't go away if you don't pay them, and in many cases *interest is still accruing.* So if you do elect to defer or forbear your loans, it is vitally important to know what you're going to do when you start making payments again.

Deferment and forbearance produce the same pause-button effect on your payments, but they are separate and distinct statuses. To qualify for deferment, your situation must fall into one of a number of clearly-defined circumstances. You can forbear your loans if you don't qualify for one of the deferment options.

For both deferment and forbearance, you must apply, and in most cases reapply, every year. Some types will only allow you to defer or forbear for a set number of years during the lifetime of your loan. Do not stop paying until you have been notified that your application was approved and that no payment is due.

The most common types of deferment are:

1. Economic hardship
2. Unemployment

3. Full or part-time school enrollment

Currently, the Department of Education website has a fantastic chart that very clearly describes the different deferment options at **studentaid.ed.gov/sa/repay-loans/deferment-forbearance**.

Should I Defer or Forbear?

Forbearance and deferment can be great strategies to integrate into your payment plan when you have a variety of debts and you want to prioritize them. Because loans in deferment or forbearance don't require a minimum payment, you can put extra cash toward a different, higher-priority loan. Just be aware that any interest you don't pay while your loans are in deferment or forbearance will be capitalized when the loans enter repayment. We're getting a little ahead of ourselves here, too, but keep that in the back of your mind as we put together your plan.

Forgiveness

If you are one of a chosen few, you may be able to benefit from grants and/or repayment assistance or have your loans forgiven entirely. Forgiveness is the Holy Grail of loan repayment, the rare exception to the rule of Paying It Off Puts You In Control. Do your research, and if you qualify for any form of forgiveness, take advantage of it.

Your loans may be forgiven if:

1. Your circumstances qualify you for a forgiveness plan; once you have made a set number of payments, your loan balance is entirely forgiven.

2. Your job qualifies you for a set amount of money to be forgiven each year.

A note on forgiveness: If you qualify for any form of federal student loan forgiveness, your one mission in life is this: DO NOT F*CK IT UP. Whatever the lenders request, give to them. If they want your tax returns, get your taxes done and submit your returns. If they want you to reapply and recertify your income every year, mark your calendar and keep a file where you compile the information as soon as you get it. If you need to make 120 or 240 on-time payments to get your loans forgiven, for the love of all that is lovely, make those effing payments on time!

And now it's student loan workout time!

Step Three (a) Workouts: Organize Your Student Loans

I commit to doing these workouts on [date(s)]: ______________________________

Workout #3a: Know Your Loans

Know your loans backwards and forwards. Call your loan company and ask, ask, ask. Keep asking for supervisors if you're not getting the answers you need.

Answer these questions for each of your loans:

1. What repayment plans am I on?
2. What is the term of each of my repayment plans?
3. Do I qualify for income-based repayment?
   * What do I need to do to qualify?
   * When do I apply?
4. Do I qualify for any forgiveness programs?
   * What do I need to do to qualify?
   * When do I apply?
5. Do I qualify for any interest-related incentives, such as a reduction for on-time payments?
   * What do I need to do to qualify?
   * When do I apply?
6. Can I get a lower interest rate?
   * What do I need to do to qualify?

- When do I apply?

7. Do I qualify for any grants or repayment assistance programs?

   - What do I need to do to qualify?
   - When do I apply?

8. Am I thinking about deferring or forbearing my student loans?

   - When will I apply?
   - What do I need to do to qualify?
   - Why am I considering this option?
   - What amount will I pay while the loans are in this status?

Some other questions I have are…

Here's how I'm going to try to find the answers:

Workout #3b: Get Organized

Set up both digital and hard copy folders to collect all the documentation related to your loans!

* Some thoughts I have about this are…

Workout #3c: Repayment Options

Research your repayment options for your student loans.

- Do I understand all the terms?
- Do I understand what I need to do to apply (and reapply)? Am I willing to make that a priority?
- Do I understand or am I willing to seek help to understand the tax implications of my plan? (This is not the time to use tax prep software!)

The plan(s) I qualify for is / are…

The plan(s) I am choosing is / are…

I am choosing this plan(s) because…

Some things I'd like to note are…

Workout #3d: Other Notes

Use this space to record notes from conversations you've had with your loan provider(s), things you have found as you've navigated the website(s) (they can be tricky!), or anything else that feels important right now.

Workout #3e: Emotional Check-In

Let's hear it!

* Before this chapter, I…

* Now I…

* I was really surprised that / by…

- My least favorite part of this chapter was…

- The best part of this chapter is…

- I'll be ready to rock this when…

By the end of this chapter you will...

- Know exactly how much your debt costs you each day.
- Understand the spending leaks that, once plugged, will put you in control.
- Be clear about your priorities.

Step Four: *analyze*

You know all that data you laid out so clearly in Chapter 3? Now we're going to examine the heck out of it and see what needs to change. You're going to ask yourself, "Hey pretty lady, what do I need to do the same or differently, right now, so I can do / be / have / feel what I want?"

This means (here come those BBDS!)...

- **Your bills.** Is there enough space after they are paid for you to feel like you can breathe, or are you spending as much as or more than you make each month? What would have to happen to create that space?
- **Your budget.** Where does your money go? Is your spending aligned with your priorities? If not, what would have to happen for that to change?
- **Your debt.** How much is it costing you? Are there interest rates you can lower?

- **Your savings.** How much do you need to feel comfortable? How much have you been saving?

- **Your priorities.** You can have everything you want. You just can't have everything. You may need to let go of one or two things to create space for something new. You'll be so much happier if you hang on to your favorites. What are your priorities and how do you rank them?

Through this hardcore exploration, your payoff plan will begin to take shape.

"Look," you may say. "I came here to take control of my debt. Why do I need to spend so much—or really *any*—time slogging through all the crap in my past and all the 'mistakes' I've made? I get it. I screwed up. This sucks. So can we please just get to the damn plan already?"

If you're thinking that, here's my response to you. A lot of financial books blab at you about debt and then go directly to the plan, do not pass go, definitely do not collect $200. But around here, we don't play like that. We look back to look forward. Here's why.

leaps up onto soapbox

Healthy, goal-oriented spending isn't about limiting yourself, it is about *paying attention*. Creating an effective debt payoff plan requires focused action and a willingness to explore your habits and history free from judgment. Saying, "Well, obviously I'm here, I'm bad with money" is *not* going to do it. Become intimately familiar with the story of your money and you will make informed decisions that lead to lasting change.

Can I give you general tips for what percentages of your money you should spend on this or that? Sure. But limiting yourself to, say, a weekly budget of 10% on this and 30% on that based on rules of thumb is like throwing a whole bunch of ingredients in a bowl and hoping a cake comes out when you bake it. On what are you going to be spending that money? How are you going to ensure you don't dip into savings or pull out your credit card? That's the work.

Looking at these numbers may make you feel guilty, sick, scared, embarrassed, sad, or something else entirely. Annnd… that's part of the point. I want to bring up *all* your sh*t, get it out there, and make something beautiful out of it.

hops off soapbox

If you're not quite ready to tackle this right now, that's OK. Here is your four-part baby action step. Ready?

1. Pull out your phone, calendar, or whatever you use to manage your schedule.

2. Set aside three hours of time at some point in the next month. It could be one hour on three days, three hours on one day, or 90 minutes on two days… you get the drift.

3. Pick the schedule that works for you, make the commitment, and hold that time sacred.

4. Ask someone else to hold you accountable. You don't even have to tell them what for. Just shoot them a quick text or e-mail and say, "Hey can you please remind me to start kicking ass on such and such day? Thanks so much!"

Put the book down and go do it. I'm so serious. You will probably never feel like doing this, so your motivation has to come from something else (i.e., your desire not to flake out on yourself, your friend, or the goals you outlined in Chapter 2).

Do it. Calendar! Right now, while you're reading and it's fresh in your mind.

I'll wait.

…

…

…

Are you back? Yay! Now let's do this.

Step Four Workouts: Analyze

I commit to doing these workouts on [date(s)]: ______________________________

Workout #4.1: Stuck in the Minimum With You + It's So Interest-ing

This workout will help you figure out how much interest you are being charged each month on your student loans and credit card debt and, correspondingly, the minimum payment you would need to make toward each of your debts each month in order to stay ahead of that interest. Don't assume that the minimum payment set by your lender covers both interest and principal.

Flip back to your Debt Overview (Workout #3.1) and use the information to complete the Minimum Payment Dominator chart as follows:

- **Lender Name / Type, Minimum Payment, Principal Balance, APR**. You should have this information in your Debt Overview. Be sure to list each debt separately in its own row!
- **Daily Interest Rate**. Divide each APR by 365 to find the daily interest rate for each of your debts. You can write this number as a decimal, a percentage, or both!
- **Daily Interest Charged**. Multiply your Principal Balance by your Daily Interest Rate to determine the amount of interest charged each day for each of your debts.
- **Monthly Interest Charged**. Multiply the Daily Interest Charged by 30 to find the total amount of interest charged each month for each of your debts.

Subtract the Monthly Interest Charged from the Minimum Payment to find out how much of your current minimum payment goes to principal and how much to interest.

We just need an estimate, not the exact number down to the penny, so don't worry about compounding vs. accruing here. An example follows, and then it's your turn!

Example: Say you have two student loans, one $30,000 at 3.65% and the other $25,000 at 7.3%, and two credit cards, one $5,000 at 14.6% and the other $6,000 at 18.25%. Here's an example of what your chart will look like when you're done:

LENDER NAME/TYPE	MINIMUM PAYMENT	PRINCIPAL BALANCE	APR	DAILY INTEREST RATE	DAILY INTEREST CHARGED	MONTHLY INTEREST CHARGED
Student Loan 1	$300.00	$30,000.00	3.65%	0.01% or 0.0001	$3.00	$90.00
Student Loan 2	$250.00	$25,000.00	7.3%	0.02% or 0.0002	$5.00	$150.00
Credit Card 1	$75.00	$5,000.00	14.6%	0.04 or 0.0004	$2.00	$60.00
Credit Card 2	$125.00	$6,000.00	18.25%	0.05% or 0.0005	$3.00	$90.00
Total	**$750.00**	**$66,000.00**			**$13.00**	**$390.00**

You can see here that the total interest charged on all four of these debts is $13 a day and nearly $400 a month! Each minimum payment is enough to cover both interest and some principal, but not much. Of the total $750 payment, less than half—$360—is paying down principal. The rest is being flushed down the interest toilet.

Again, this is not to make you feel bad! You need to know this so that you can decide what to do about it.

Now it's your turn...

Minimum Payment Dominator

LENDER NAME/ TYPE	MINIMUM PAYMENT	PRINCIPAL BALANCE	APR	DAILY INTEREST RATE	DAILY INTEREST CHARGED	MONTHLY INTEREST CHARGED
Total						

Interest Rates

- I will attempt to lower the interest rate on my ______________________ by…

- The steps I need to take to do this are…

- I commit to doing this by _______________ *(date)*

* The result of my attempt was…

* Here's how I feel about the result…

Minimum Payment

- ✱ I will attempt to lower the minimum payment on my _______________ by…

- ✱ The steps I need to take to do this are…

- ✱ I commit to doing this by _______________ *(date)*

- The result of my attempt was…

- Here's how I feel about the result…

Workout #4.2: Spending "Reality Check"

There are two steps to creating a realistic budget or spending plan that will help you pay off your debt. This workout addresses the first step; we'll tackle the second step in the next chapter.

In Workout #3.3 you created a list of how you spent your money during the last three months and assigned a category to each transaction. Using that list, we're now going to create a "reality check" that reflects the reality of your spending now. Without this foundation, you risk creating a spending plan that that is so far from your current reality you can't make it stick. People don't successfully transition from eating a four-course steak dinner every night to eating only carrots at every meal. Let's not set you up to feel horrible from the get-go.

Don't cheat. These are just numbers; they don't mean anything about you.

Continuing to kick it old school here, you're going to need a calculator and either the Average Spending Playsheet on the next page or a spreadsheet that's set up to look like that playsheet (if you're comfortable using one).

Here's how to fill in your Average Spending Playsheet:

1. List your eight to twelve categories in alphabetical order (just to keep things nice and tidy!).

2. Go through the Spending Round-Up you created in Workout #3.3, one category at a time, and add up the total spent in each category.

3. Write the number of months you're counting. If you gathered three months of expenses, the number you'd write in each row is "3."

4. If you have some additional expenses that only occur a couple of times a year that weren't captured, you can include those, too. For example, if you pay car insurance twice a year, one payment covers six months, so you'd write "6."

5. Divide the total by the months counted to find the average for each category.

Average Spending Playsheet

CATEGORY	TOTAL	# MONTHS COUNTED	AVERAGE

Now, we will use the numbers from this Playsheet to create your Reality Check.

The Reality Check (and, eventually, your spending plan) has six columns:

1. **Category**: The eight to twelve from the previous page plus the categories from your Bills worksheet in Workout #3.2.

2. **Income**: All the money that flows in—each source should have its own row.

3. **Bills**: Your fixed expenses each month (taken directly from Workout #3.2).

4. **Variable**: The numbers corresponding to the spending categories each month (be sure not to double-count bills!).

5. **Total**: The sum of all these numbers.

6. **Notes**: Anything else you would like to include.

There are three separate columns for income, bills, and expenses so that you can easily total up each type at the bottom. Once you have all three numbers at the bottom, calculate your total income minus your bills and variable expenses. This will tell you if you are spending more than you are bringing in, and by how much. Your goal is a positive total number, but be aware that you may not get one at first—and that's fine. Remember, as with everything else, we need to know where you are now in order to know where you need to go and how to get there.

A note about food: Food-related expenses should be divided into at least three different categories. If you are like most people, there are three distinct ways you experience the acts of purchasing and eating food. One, the groceries you buy and bring home to prepare or cook. Two, the quick service or fast food meals you grab and eat on the go, which usually include breakfasts, lunches, and snacks. Three, the restaurant meals you share with others, reveling in lively conversation over food and drink brought to your table.

Depending on your lifestyle, you may also add a takeout or order-in category, a category for snacks, and/or a category for drinks. Don't go nuts with this, but the point is, you get to decide and your categories should be reflective of the various ways that you enjoy food in your life.

Here's an example of a completed Reality Check; a blank one follows.

CATEGORY	INCOME	BILLS	VARIABLE	TOTAL	NOTES
PAYDAY (net)	**$4,000.00**				
SAVINGS		$0.00			Obviously want to increase this!
Credit Card Debt		$175.00			
Student Loan Debt		$800.00			
Rent / Mortgage		$1,200.00			
Insurance		$54.00			$650 per year = $54 per month
Electric / Gas		$75.00			
Phone		$100.00			
Cable / Internet		$150.00			
Car		$0.00			
Subway		$0.00			
Gym		$100.00			
Apparel			$120.00		
Cash			$60.00		
Donations / Charity			$10.00		
Entertainment			$87.00		
Grocery			$300.00		
Health / Beauty			$80.00		
Medical			$50.00		
Meals - Fast Food			$200.00		
Meals - Restaurant			$360.00		
Transportation			$45.00		
Travel			$300.00		
Miscellaneous			$20.00		
TOTAL	**$4,000.00**	**$2,654.00**	**$1,632.00**	**-$262.00**	<== Your goal is a positive number here!

Now it's your turn to have at it...

Reality Check

CATEGORY	INCOME	BILLS	VARIABLE	TOTAL	NOTES
PAYDAY (net)					
SAVINGS					

Reality Check, Continued

CATEGORY	INCOME	BILLS	VARIABLE	TOTAL	NOTES
TOTAL					<== Your goal is a positive number here!

Tip #1: If you're comfortable creating your own spreadsheet, the formulas for the totals are basic "=SUM" formulas. If you are iffy with spreadsheets, don't worry about this at all! The spreadsheet will automate some of the math for you but you can do this just as easily using a calculator.

Tip #2: Remember, any categories that don't apply to you don't need to be there—ths is *my* template designed become *your* reality check!

Workout #4.3: Patterns, Habits, Surprises

Every time you spend or don't spend your money, you're making a choice. The more you understand your choices, the more consciously, confidently, and powerfully you will make them.

Take a few minutes to journal through these questions as you refelect on your Reality Check:

- What patterns emerged for you?

- What habits or spending patterns surprised you in a bad way?

* What habits or spending patterns surprised you in a good way?

* What habits or spending patterns did not surprise you?

* What upset you?

* What made you feel awesome / proud?

The things that surprised you in a bad way are the places you're leaking money. We'll look at this in more detail in the next workout.

Workout #4.4: Super Sleuth Time: Identifying Leaks

Here are some prompts to help you identify your priorities:

- These items / categories are non-negotiable necessities:

- These items / categories aren't non-negotiable necessities in the food-clothing-shelter-oxygen sense, but they make me really happy:

Here are some prompts to help you identify where money is leaking:

- These items are non-negotiable necessities, but I really wish they weren't:

✱ I had completely forgotten about these items:

✱ I don't even know what these items are:

✱ I feel really guilty about having spent money on these items:

- I returned these items for money back or store credit (if you got money back, be sure to capture that in your Reality Check as it reduces the amount spent in that category!):

- I meant to return these items for money back and I straight up didn't / forgot:

- I didn't realize I spent so much money at these stores / places or on these items, even when I didn't intend to:

And finally, here are some clues as to how your spending may not be in line with your priorities:

- Even though I would love to, I never or rarely spend money on:

- I never feel like I have the money to / for:

If you'd like to take it one step further, go through your Spending Round-Up and highlight or put a star next to the items that made you feel happy so you can see when your spending is aligned with your happiness and when it isn't.

Workout #4.5: Identifying Your Priorities

Re-visit your "So I can...."s from Workout #2.1. Have they changed?

The top three goals paying off my debt will help me achieve:

Goal #1:

Goal #2:

Goal #3:

Now, spend five to ten minutes journaling your answers to these prompts:

- What am I willing and not willing to give up to achieve my goals?

* What are my basic needs (non-negotiable)?

* What do I need in my life to stay sane / happy?

* What will I need to feel secure about my future?

And now it's time to prioritize. We want you filling your life with the things that are most important to you.

My top five priorities are:

- **Priority #1:**

- **Priority #2:**

- **Priority #3:**

- **Priority #4:**

- **Priority #5:**

Workout #4.6: Emotional Check-In

Because being on top of money is about what you do *and* how you feel, let's check in. How do you feel about what you accomplished in this chapter?

- Before this chapter I…

- Now I…

- The most helpful / effective portion of this chapter for me was…

- The least helpful / effective portion of this chapter for me was…

- I was really surprised that / by...

- The three questions this chapter raised for me are…

- My #1 takeaway from this chapter is…

- I also want to note that…

Workout # 4.7: Play Date!

NOW GO PLAY.

If you need to collapse on the couch right now, do it. But tomorrow, get up and put something physical in your calendar. Karaoke (my favorite!), yoga, a swim, a run, a dance party in front of your mirror, even a long walk around your neighborhood. Rock that playlist, venture out in the world, breathe, and *absorb*! I'm one of the least athletic people ever, and even I'm telling you that this is *not* the time to de-stress with a Netflix marathon. Get moving and get awesome.

You are *doing* this.

For support and bonus resources to accompany these workouts, come hang out at **OweLessLiveMore.com**!

In this chapter we're going to tie it all together with a big red shiny bow. You're going to decide...

- When you will have your debt paid off.
- In what order you will pay off your debt.
- How much savings you need to feel safe and comfortable.
- How you will create the money you need each month to hit your target payoff date and build savings.

This is really the meat-and-potatoes (or the equivalent vegan option, if that's your style) of dominating your debt.

Step Five: *plan*

Having a plan to pay off your debt means (1) you have a target date, (2) you know how much you need to put toward your debt each month to hit that date, (3) you are able to put that much money toward your debt each month, and (4) you are able to balance that with setting aside money for savings.

To create your plan, you have five major decisions to make:

1. When do you want your debt to be paid off?
2. In what order will you attack your debts?
3. What amount will you pay each month?
4. How do you want to balance paying off your debt with building savings?
5. What sacrifices are you willing (and not willing) to make to reach your goals?

We'll go through how to make each of these decisions first. Then, in the workouts that follow, you will actually decide.

Choice One: Target Date

Start with what you want. How soon do you want to get rid of your debt? Don't worry about what is realistic yet. Go with your gut and what *feels* like a good date, and we'll let the numbers take it from there.

Choice Two: Order

If you have more than one debt—multiple credit cards, multiple student loans, etc.—you get to choose the order in which you pay them off. Having several debts means you have several options. All debts are not created equal; some of your debts are indeed worse than others. The sooner you get rid of the worst ones the easier it is to attack the rest.

If you don't actively choose the order in which to pay off your debts, the default is usually to spread payments across all of your debts equally. For most people, giving equal weight to each debt makes the least amount of emotional and financial sense because you are not targeting the worst debts first. If you do elect to spread your payments across all debts equally, let's be sure it is a conscious choice.

You can pay off your debts according to interest rate, size, emotional charge, or some combination of these. Other factors specific to student loans include whether the loan is federal or private and whether the loan is subsidized or unsubsidized.

The chart below will help you determine which debts are higher priority and which are lower.

TYPE OF DEBT	PRIORITY	WHY
High interest	Higher	Carrying high interest debt costs you the most amount of money in the long run.
Smallest	Higher	Smaller debts are easier to pay off, giving you a motivational sense of accomplishment.
Most emotionally-charged	Higher	Emotionally-charged debt causes stress.
Variable interest rate	Higher	Variable interest rates cause feelings of uncertainty (and stress).
Private student loans	Higher	Private loans have less payment flexibility than public loans.
Unsubsidized student loans	Higher	Carrying unsubsidized loans costs you more money in the long run than subsidized loans.
Low(er) interest	Lower	Lower interest rates cost you less money over time compared with higher interest debts.
Largest	Lower	Larger debts take longer to get rid of; that feeling of "chipping away" can be frustrating.
Least emotionally charged	Lower	These debts don't cause you as much stress as their counterparts.
Fixed interest rate	Lower	Fixed interest rates provide stability (even if a variable interest rate happens to be lower).
Federal student loans	Lower	There are more repayment options than with private loans.
Subsidized student loans	Lower	Interest will be covered in certain instances of non-repayment (deferment or forbearance).

Weighing all these factors, you will be able to decide in what order to pay off your debt. You will probably find that your credit cards are highest priority, your student loans are next, and your mortgage and car loan come last, but that is not always true, so it's important to do this analysis for yourself! We will take a close look at this in the workouts.

Choice Three: Payment Amount

To determine how much to pay, you will need to know:

1. The minimum your lender requires you to pay each month (and whether that amount can be lowered).

2. The amount of interest you are charged each month.

3. The reality of your income and spending, and what adjustments you are willing and able to make to bring that reality into alignment with your goals.

Let's go through each of these in detail.

1. **What is the minimum you have to pay each month?**

Your lenders have effectively created a payment plan for you by giving you a minimum amount to pay each month. When you take on debt, you commit to paying that amount or you risk default and other unpleasantries. Stay on top of your minimum payments, and you control the rest.

Note that you are not stuck with whatever minimum payment your lender has given you. Your lender wants to get its money back and would rather have you pay something than nothing at all. You and your lender may be able to reach a different agreement regarding your minimum payment.

The lower your minimum payment, the more flexibility you have over how to allocate your money across your debts. A lower minimum payment does not mean you are off the hook, it just gives you more control over the order in which you repay. Refinancing, consolidating, switching repayment plans, deferring or forbearing federal student loans, and settling your debt for less than what you owe will lower your minimum payment, but these are advanced strategies. Use them only once you have a well-thought-out plan in place.

Consolidating

"Consolidating" means "lumping all your loans into one debt with one payment and one interest rate that is the average of all your interest rates." It usually spreads the payments out over a longer time period, lowering your monthly payment. Consolidation is a form of refinancing; true loan consolidation is only available for federal student loans.

Reasons to consolidate your loans include:

- Certainty: Securing a fixed interest rate on loans with variable interest rates
- Flexibility: Lowering your monthly payment by extending the repayment term
- Convenience: Combining a series of debts with all different due dates into one debt with one monthly payment

Should you consolidate? It depends. The most common trap with consolidation is the false sense of saving. Because the new interest rate in a loan consolidation is generally a weighted average of all your previous interest rates, you're not paying less interest. Your minimum payment will likely be (much) lower, but that's because the repayment term has been extended. With a consolidation loan, if you take the full term to pay it off, you may make double (or more!) the original number of payments. Tack interest onto that, and your debt has suddenly become much, much more expensive.

But there are many positive aspects of consolidating, too. Consolidating variable-interest loans to secure a fixed interest rate on the lower end of the spectrum will absolutely save you money. Consolidating multiple loans with different due dates into a single payment will save you time (and help you stay organized!). Finally, extending your repayment term to lower your monthly minimum payment gives you a lot more flexibility. If your consolidated debt is lower on your repayment priority list, the lower minimum payment gives you the opportunity to focus on your higher-priority debts first and come back to your consolidated debt later.

Example:

You have three loans, each on a ten-year repayment plan:

- $17,500 at 10% interest
- $10,500 at 7.5% interest
- $7,000 at 5% interest

When you consolidate these three loans, you get a $35,000 loan, and your repayment plan is extended to 20 years with an interest rate of 8.25%.

The 8.25% interest rate on the new loan is the average of 10%, 7.5% and 5%, weighted according to the size of the original loans corresponding to each rate. So you can see that while the original 10% interest rate decreased by 1.75%, the 5% interest rate increased by 3.5%!

So. Consolidation may make sense as part of your plan, but not if it's your whole plan.

Refinancing

"Refinancing" is a fancy term that means "paying off your debt with another debt."

Most people think of refinancing in the context of mortgages because that's where the term is most often used, but it is actually much broader than that. Technically, any time you pay off one debt with another debt, you are refinancing. Transferring one credit card balance to a different credit card with a lower interest rate? Refinancing. Borrowing from your retirement account? Refinancing. Taking out an equity line of credit to pay off your credit card? Refinancing.

Should you refinance? It depends. When you refinance, yes, you are generally getting a lower interest rate and/or lower minimum payment. That part is great! The problem is, most people stop there, don't ask the rest of the questions, and end up in a worse position than if they had stayed the course with their original debt. Refinancing can make financial sense. But very often it's the gateway into the Stinky Cycle of Debt. Here's what you need to know to refinance (or not) with confidence and stay out of the Stinky Cycle.

Fixed Payment Plan: When you refinance a loan with a set number of payments, such as a mortgage, private student loan, or similar debt, you may get a lower interest rate, but you also effectively start over. There are two things to know. One, you will probably pay a fee for that privilege. Two, your minimum payment will be lower when you refinance not because your new lender is so generous, but because your new lender has reset the clock on your payment plan. Here's an example to show how that can work against you.

Example:

Let's say your original loan was $12,000 and you are on a ten-year plan, paying $100 per month or $1,200 per year in principal. (This is not realistic because there would be interest and a loan like this would likely be amortized, but we're ignoring that for the purpose of this example.)

After four years you have paid off $4,800, leaving you with $7,200 spread out over the six remaining years. You refinance by taking out a new ten-year loan for the $7,200. Now you have ten years to pay off $7,200 so you've lowered your monthly payment to $60 ($7,200 divided by 120 months) instead of $100.

Hooray! Except you've also extended the length of time you'll be in debt—and paying interest—from a total of ten years to a total of fourteen years. So yes, you've locked in a lower monthly payment, but you'll be paying interest for longer, which means you will likely spend a lot more money on this debt.

Does refinancing your mortgage (or similar debt) make sense for you? Here's your **Loan Refinancing Pop Quiz**. Answer these questions True or False:

_____ This particular debt is a lower priority for me and I am refinancing it as part of my overall debt domination strategy.

_____ I have done the math and the new interest rate is low enough to offset the fees and/or the total amount I will pay over the new extended repayment period.

_____ I intend to pay off my refinanced debt in less time than the new extended repayment period allows, so I will end up paying less than I would have under the old terms.

If you answered "true" to any one of these, refinancing may make sense for you.

No Fixed Payment Plan: Refinancing your credit card debt by transferring your balance to a 0% card will result in either a happy dance of debt domination or a gloppy swamp of horror and misery. There are two really, really important things you need to know if you want to employ this strategy and end up dancing.

One, you must bust out a magnifying glass and read the fine print. Every offer is different and there may be some scary sh*t in there you need to know about before it bites you in the ass. With credit card transfers, the 0% interest rate is always promotional. That means it is going to expire, usually in twelve to eighteen months.

When the promotional period is over, the credit card company can give you whatever interest rate they want, and it's probably going to be high. No matter what the offer letter says, the credit card company does this not to reward you because they think you're so awesome, but to lure you in so they can make money off you.

For example, the promotional interest rate may apply only to balances transferred within a certain period of time, not to all transfers during the promotional period. It also often applies only to the transferred balance, not to new purchases made with the card. In other words, if you use the card to buy things and don't pay them off in full, you may pay interest on them. Each offer is different. Read the fine print.

Two, when you pay off your card(s) using the 0% card as part of your debt domination strategy, you must stop creating debt on all of your other cards. You're done. Period. Last stop, everyone off the debt train. Otherwise, what's going to happen is this (and trust me, I know this because I have heard it so many times):

You'll see $0 balances on all those cards on which you're so used to seeing balances. You will feel like you've gotten a fresh start. It will be thrilling. And then something will come up and you'll use the card "just this once." And then it will happen again. And again. And you'll start to get nervous and stop looking at your statements because you know it's bad and you don't really want to know how bad. And now, not only are you not making enough of a dent in the 0% card, you're not paying off the other cards either. When the promotional period expires, you haven't paid off the card, and now you have high interest, unsecured debt on yet another credit card. And the Stinky Cycle continues.

Does transferring your credit card balance(s) make sense for you? Here's your **Credit Card Refinancing Pop Quiz**. Answer these questions True or False:

_______ I have a plan and I know I will be able to pay off the balance before the promotional period ends. (Note: "I know I will" is different from "I hope to" or "I'd like to" or even "I'm pretty sure I will be able to.")

_______ The fees I will pay to transfer the balance are less than what I will pay in interest on my current card(s) during the promotional period.

_______ I have the cash to support my lifestyle while I am paying off the 0% interest credit card without adding to my balance on any other credit cards.

_______ I have read the fine print and know the terms that apply to this offer.

If you answered "true" to all four of these questions, transferring your balance may make sense for you.

Refinancing is a tool, not a solution. Paying off your debt with debt won't make it go away. The only thing that will make your debt go away is CASH. When you refinance, you have just as much debt as you did before. You can absolutely integrate it into your plan, just understand that refinancing itself is not a plan. Do your research, keep your eyes open, and go for it only if it makes sense.

2. **How much interest accrues each month?**

Hard truth: If you are only keeping up with the "thank you fee" YOU ARE NOT MAKING A DENT IN YOUR DEBT. Sorry for yelling, but you must hear this loud and clear!

When you make a payment, the money is applied first to fees, then to interest, then to principal. This is why, for many people (and maybe even for you), making payment after payment never seems to make a dent in the balance. I'll refrain from hopping back up onto my soapbox again, but this has been a huge problem in the consumer lending industry. Predatory lenders lock unsuspecting borrowers into loans with low! low! low! monthly payments that are 100% interest. Your payments need to be high enough to cover fees (of which there are hopefully none), interest, *and* principal. Higher payments → Bigger dent in the principal → Less interest paid → More money to put toward principal → Debt paid off with less money.

Calculating your interest costs per month as we did in Workout #4.1 is the first step to figuring out what you need to pay to attack that principal. As with your minimum payment, you are not necessarily stuck with the first interest rate your lender gives you. Ultimately, your lender just wants to keep you merrily paying along. If you ask nicely (or if you refinance), your lender may agree to give you a lower rate.

3. **How much money can you put toward your debt each month?**

The spending workouts you have done up to this point have given you an answer to this question. If you're not happy with that answer—that is, if the amount of money you have to put toward your debt each month isn't enough to get you where you want to be—here are your alternatives:

- Make more
- Spend less
- Push out your target date
- Keep everything the same… and freaking own it

I have yet to encounter one person (including me!) who hasn't had to embrace at least one of these techniques to make their payment plan work.

Choice Four: How Much to Save?

Dominating your debt is about balance, specifically:

- Paying as little interest as possible
- Living a life that doesn't completely suck
- Building up savings

Throwing everything you have at your debt means you won't have savings. That's no good because, as you know, savings is the key to staying out of the Stinky Cycle of Debt.

If your financial situation makes you anxious but you can't put your finger on why, the culprit is just as likely related to savings as to debt.

You need both cash savings and retirement (investment) savings. Not because I said so, but because having money in the bank and invested for your future will make you feel amazing—and give you a hell of a lot of confidence. Remember the money pyramid? Savings provides something that is extremely valuable to well-rounded, happy humans: *safety*.

Having money in the bank is like putting a big, cozy mattress between you and the floor. If you have no income for a while, savings gives you a little room and time to get back on your feet. If a situation should arise that calls for immediate action, you can do what you need to do and get where you need to go without having to worry about where to get the money. Most importantly, having savings means that if something comes up that costs money, *you will not have to go into debt to pay for it*. You can buy it, have it, love it, and still have money left.

In short, having a significant chunk of savings gives you options and a level of control that debt does not.

Should I borrow from (or cash out) my retirement account?

As a general rule, the answer is "NO... unless."

Cashing out? Bright line rule here: don't. When you cash out all or even a portion of your retirement account, you pay huge penalties. You also lose out—big time—on the income and growth of the account. That money needs to be there as long as humanly possible, or it's not going to grow. And if you're going to be living off that money for twenty years, you really, really, really need it to grow so you'll have enough money when you retire.

Borrowing? Grayer area. When you borrow against your 401(k) or IRA, you may get a lower interest rate than whatever you're paying on your credit cards or student loan debt. So this can make sense for you... IF (IF! IF! IF! IF! IF!) you are getting a lower rate, you're not paying penalties, you're not losing out on the income and growth, and, most importantly, you know *exactly* how you're going to pay it off.

My best advice to you? If you really, really want to use investments to pay off debt, talk to a financial professional first. Otherwise don't f*ck with your retirement account. It is not cash. It is not free money. Pretend it's not there. Put money in it and forget about it. You will be very happy you did.

Choice Five: Priorities and Sacrifices

Prioritizing your debt over other things may suck. You may hate it. Or it may not be so terrible at all! Whatever the case, remember that being in debt is a temporary situation. Paying it off takes time and discipline, but you wield a lot of power, and you can choose what to do or not do.

Here is a suggestion for how to rank your priorities:

1. Your bills (including debt minimum payment).
2. Your savings account.
3. Your sanity.
4. Your debt (extra payments).
5. Everything else.

Ranking your priorities is like packing for a vacation. You pick a bunch of things based on the weather where you're going, what's comfortable, what you're going to do there, etc. You don't throw the rest of your clothes in the garbage; you just don't take them with you right now. If you have more debt than money to pay it right now, you need to hone in on what you most want to take with you and leave the rest for when you get back. You get to choose.

Yes, this may be unpleasant at first. But it will also give you tremendous focus as you determine what's really most important to you. And at the end, you will replace the burden of your debt with lightness, freedom, and relief.

The Rules: Following the Script and Finding Sucess

Your plan is actually pretty simple, isn't it? Find or create extra cash, allocate some to savings and some to debt, be patient, and stick with it.

The "rules" that will help you pay off your debt as quickly as possible are:

1. Lower your minimum payment as much as possible without incurring any penalties.

2. Stay ahead of the interest.

3. Have a target date.

4. Go slow and steady; resist the urge to throw everything at your debt.

5. Live within your means (by making more or spending less), and put money into savings and leave it there.

All the calculations, soul-searching, and hard work you've done can be boiled down to one final question: if what I want is to pay off my debt, what am I willing to give up (or not) to get there?

Let's work this out.

Step Five Workouts: Plan

I commit to doing these workouts on [date(s)]: ______________________

Workout #5.1: Debt Payoff Goals

Fill in the blanks:

- The total debt I have is $______________________.
- I want it paid off by (*date*)__________________ which is in __________ months.
- Right now I can put $______________________ toward my debt each month on top of the interest.
- Right now I can put $______________________ into savings each month.
- By the time my debt is paid off, I want to have $______________________ in savings.

Don't self-edit. In the rest of the workouts, we will figure out if what you want can work, and if not, what needs to happen to make sure your goals are realistic. For now, just answer from your heart.

Example: You have $18,000 in credit card debt. You really want to pay it off in 18 months and have $6,300 in savings. You're prepared to put $800 toward the principal each month, and $200 into savings.

- The total debt I have is $18,000.
- I want it paid off by next July which is in 18 months.
- Right now I can put $800 toward my debt each month on top of the interest.
- Right now I can put $200 into savings each month.
- By the time my debt is paid off, I want to have $6,300 in savings.

These numbers give you a starting point to figure out your options, which will almost always be either (1) create more money, or (2) push out your target date. The next two activities will help you determine which one of these is right for you.

Option One: Create more money

Fill in the blanks!

My Goal: To pay off $_____________ in debt and save $_____________ over the course of _____ months

* The amount I need to put toward my debt principal each month is $________. (*divide the amount of your principal by the number of months*)
* The amount I need to put into savings each month is $__________________.
* The total needed each month is $_____________.
* Right now I have $_____________ available.
* To hit my target date, I need to find a way to create an extra $_____________ per month.

Example: My goal: To pay off $18,000 in debt and save $6,300 over the course of 18 months.

* The amount I need to put toward my debt principal each month is $1,000.
* The amount I need to put into savings each month is $350.
* The total needed each month is $1,350.
* Right now I have $1,000 available.
* To hit my target date, I need to find a way to create an extra $350 per month.

Option Two: Push out your target date

Fill in more blanks!

My Goal: To pay off $____________ in debt and save $____________ over the course of ____ months.

- My total debt principal is $____________.
- Right now I have $____________ available to put toward my debt principal each month.
- If I put that amount towards my debt each month, it will take me ______ months to pay off my debt. (*divide the amount of your debt principal by the payment amount*)
- Right now I have $____________ available to put into savings each month.
- If I put that amount into savings each month, by the time my debt is paid off I will have $____________ in savings. (*multiply the savings amount by the number of months until your debt is paid off*)
- It will take me an additional ____ months to hit my savings goal.

Example: My goal: To pay off $18,000 in debt and save $6,000 over the course of 18 months.

- My total debt principal is $18,000.
- Right now I have $800 available to put toward my debt principal each month, so it will take me 23 months to pay off my debt.
- Right now I have $200 available to put into savings each month, so by the time my debt is paid off I will have $4,600 in savings.
- Once my debt is paid off, I will have an extra $800 each month. If I contribute that to savings on top of the $200 I have always been contributing, I will hit my savings goal in 3 more months!

So! Here's where you get to make some powerful decisions that will show you where to focus your energy.

* Determined to hit your target date? Your work will be to figure out how to create the extra money per month you need.
* See no possible way to create extra money? Your tunnel has a bright light shining at the end of it and you know exactly how far away it is—own it!

Answer the questions from your heart, and then use your head to make it work. Once you have your ideal scenario, try it out. Create it, tweak it until it works, and commit to it. Track your progress and re-evaluate. Lather, rinse, repeat.

Let's summarize.

* The amount I actually need per month if I want to pay off my debt by my target date is: $______________.
* The number of months (or years) it will take me to pay off my debt if I stick with the amount of money I think I can put toward it each month is ______ .

Here are the steps I will take to do this:

Workout #5.2: Order Up!

This workout will help you determine in what order to pay off your debt based on what will be easiest / least expensive / most effective for you.

List all your debts, the minimum payment, the percent interest, the principal balance, whether the interest rate is fixed or variable, whether the loan is subsidized or unsubsidized (student loans), and whether the debt is secured or unsecured.

Now, rank them. Assign each of your debts a number from 1 to *x* (where *x* is the number of debts you have) in each of three categories, as follows:

- **Size:** Largest (1) to smallest (*x*) principal balance
- **Interest:** Lowest (1) to highest (*x*) interest rate
- **Emotion:** Lowest (1) to highest (*x*) emotional charge

Then determine whether the debt is…

- **Fixed or variable?** Assign a 1 to all debt for which the interest rate is fixed, and *x* to all debt for which the interest rate is variable.
- **Subsidized or unsubsidized?** Assign a 1 to federal student loans that are subsidized, and *x* to all other debt.
- **Secured or unsecured?** Assign a 1 to federal student loans and/or secured debt, and *x* to private student loans and/or unsecured debt (including credit cards).

Once you have assigned all these numbers, add them up. The debt with the highest "score" is likely to be your highest priority, the debt with the next highest score is your next highest priority, and so on. (See! Aren't numbers wonderful?)

Here's an example of how your completed chart might look:

DEBT	MINIMUM PAYMENT	% INTEREST	PRINCIPAL BALANCE	SIZE RANK
Federal Student Loan (unsub)	$300.00	8.5%	$40,000.00	2
Federal Student Loan (sub)	$200.00	7.5%	$30,000.00	3
Private Student Loan	$600.00	3.5%	$100,000.00	1
Credit Card	$100.00	12.0%	$10,000.00	4

Now it's your turn.

Debt Paydown Priorities

DEBT	MINIMUM PAYMENT	% INTEREST	PRINCIPAL BALANCE	SIZE RANK

INTEREST RANK	EMOTIONAL RANK	FIXED OR VARIABLE?	SUBSIDIZED OR UNSUBSIDIZED?	SECURED OR UNSECURED?	TOTAL SCORE
3	2	1	4	1	13
2	1	1	1	1	9
1	4	4	4	4	18
4	3	4	4	4	23

INTEREST RANK	EMOTIONAL RANK	FIXED OR VARIABLE?	SUBSIDIZED OR UNSUBSIDIZED?	SECURED OR UNSECURED?	TOTAL SCORE

Workout #5.3: Making More

This workout will help you concretize how you can make more money. Here are the main places "make more" is hanging out:

1. Your current job.
2. Another job(s).
3. Low-hanging fruit (reimbursements, collecting money you are owed).
4. Stuff you own.
5. Gifts.

Are *all* of these doable or obtainable for you? Probably not. But they are your options. I urge you to think through each one carefully to decide whether it's a good option for you.

Remember, this phase of placing your debt front and center is *temporary*. Your target date is a bright, shining light at the end of the tunnel! You only have to make it that far and then you're free. Take it one day at a time. Refer to the list you brainstormed in Workout #3.6 for inspiration.

* The top three things I can do to make more money are…

* The easiest one for me would be…

- The first step I will take is…

The date by which I commit to taking that step is:

- The next step I will take is…

The date by which I commit to taking that step is:

- The next step I will take is…

The date by which I commit to taking that step is:

- The next step I will take is…

The date by which I commit to taking that step is:

- The next step I will take is…

The date by which I commit to taking that step is:

Workout #5.4: Spending Less + Your Spending Plan

Here are the main places "spend less" is hanging out:

1. **Your bills**

   * Bills that are level or exactly the same each month (subscriptions, etc.)
   * Bills for which the payment amount varies, but the fact that it's coming doesn't (electricity, water, etc.)

2. **Necessary consumable expenses**

   * Expenses that are somewhat within your control and directly related to how much you consume, such as gas, groceries, repairs, transportation

3. **Discretionary expenses**

   * Items and services you don't need for survival (food, clothing, shelter) but that are pretty dang important to you; the amount you spend is entirely within your control

4. **Debt**

   * As you pay it off, you will free up money not only from the principal but from the interest you won't pay. HOORAY!

5. **Savings / investing**

   * The celebrated "pay yourself first," this is a very necessary expense

When you create your Spending Plan, you are deciding, based on how much you *do* spend (your Reality Check), how much you *should* spend. Use your Spending Plan as your guide to making spending decisions.

Turning your Reality Check into your Spending Plan is like doing a puzzle where the pieces are your numbers. Add money to your payday. Cut expenses that surprised you (or that don't seem as important as paying off your debt). Use your priorities list to help make decisions. Include what you can for savings. Every dollar has a part to play. Move numbers around, flip them sideways, keep looking at the big picture, and stick with it until everything fits together and the bottom number is above $0. Stop when you're satisfied.

Create your new spending plan on the next pages!

Spending Plan!

CATEGORY	INCOME	BILLS	VARIABLE	TOTAL	NOTES
PAYDAY (net)					
SAVINGS					

Spending Plan, Continued

CATEGORY	INCOME	BILLS	VARIABLE	TOTAL	NOTES
TOTAL					<== Your goal is a positive number here!

Workout #5.5: How Much Savings Do I Need?

How much savings do you need? The general rule of thumb is three to six months of income. The logic behind that rule is, if something happened to your income, three to six months is roughly how long it would take you to find replacement income.

Now that you understand that rule of thumb, forget about it. We're going to do a different test and find a different number I like to call your "Snug-as a-Bug Number." This number is a range based on what you spend, not on what you earn, and it is the number that will help you sleep at night.

There's no right way to sleep. The only requirement is that you *get sleep* or you can't function. How much and in what way is up to you. What makes you feel snug as a bug? Maybe you like the AC on in the winter. Maybe you have the heat on and kick off the blankets. Maybe you sleep naked, or in silk matching pajamas, or a tank top and boxers. Maybe you can't sleep unless the TV is on, or maybe you need complete silence.

Picking up what I'm putting down?

Just like there's no right way to sleep, there's no right way to save. With that in mind, because sleeping comes naturally to most people and saving doesn't, here are some questions to help you find your optimal level of comfort when it comes to savings.

- **Question #1:** If tomorrow you needed $5,000 more than you have now, where would you get it?

Your reaction to this question will give you some clues about how much savings will make you comfortable. Are you a hustler, baby? Are you okay with the idea of ruthlessly slashing your expenses? Is it easy for you to rely on the generosity of family and friends? If yes, this question probably didn't faze you, and you will be comfortable on the lower end of the range. If, however, you were horrified and defeated by this question, you will feel more comfortable on the higher end. Think about the evidence from your past and make sure you're facing the reality of the way things are and not the dream of the way you wish they were.

✷ **Question #2:** Pop Quiz! How highly do you value control, independence, and freedom? Answer these questions True or False:

____ I consider myself spontaneous.

____ I like things done a certain way.

____ If I want something done right, I usually have to do it myself.

____ I tend to hang onto the things I cherish.

____ I hate to get rid of things.

____ I like to figure things out for myself.

____ I don't like being told what to do.

____ I hate to ask for help.

If you answered "true" to five or more questions, then you have a high Control, Independence, and Freedom (CIF) score, which means these are high values for you. Your Snug-as-a-Bug number is likely on the higher end of the savings spectrum.

Some thoughts I have about this are...

Finding Your Snug-as-a-Bug Savings Number

Flip back to either your Reality Check or your spending plan. What is the average total amount you spend or plan to spend each month? Find that number, and then highlight or circle your Snug-as-a-Bug range here:

YOUR SPENDING	SNUG-AS-A-BUG RANGE		
AMOUNT SPENT PER MONTH	3 MONTHS	6 MONTHS	12 MONTHS
$1,500	$4,500	$9,000	$18,000
$2,000	$6,000	$12,000	$24,000
$2,500	$7,500	$15,000	$30,000
$3,000	$9,000	$18,000	$36,000
$3,500	$10,500	$21,000	$42,000
$4,000	$12,000	$24,000	$48,000
$4,500	$13,500	$27,000	$54,000
$5,000	$15,000	$30,000	$60,000
$5,500	$16,500	$33,000	$66,000
$6,000	$18,000	$36,000	$72,000
$6,500	$19,500	$39,000	$78,000
$7,000	$21,000	$42,000	$84,000
$7,500	$22,500	$45,000	$90,000
$8,000	$24,000	$48,000	$96,000
$8,500	$25,500	$51,000	$102,000
$9,000	$27,000	$54,000	$108,000
$9,500	$28,500	$57,000	$114,000
$10,000	$30,000	$60,000	$120,000
$10,500	$31,500	$63,000	$126,000
$11,000	$33,000	$66,000	$132,000
$11,500	$34,500	$69,000	$138,000
$12,000	$36,000	$72,000	$144,000

Example: Based on your Reality Check, you spend an average of $5,000 each month. If you're a hustler, not terribly risk-averse, and have a lower CIF score, you will feel cuddled up and cozy with about $15,000 in your savings account.

If you are less of a hustler and have a higher CIF score, your Snug-as-a-Bug number jumps to $60,000. Again, we're talking cash here—this is in addition to any amounts you have invested and/or in a retirement account.

If you are thinking, "OMG yikes bikes, you crazy woman!" remember, this isn't how much money you must have saved up or the evil money monster will come smite you in the middle of the night. This is just my loving recommendation. This amount will help you sleep like a princess on a mattress made of money.

Yes, that is a real number, and yes that number is achievable. Maybe it feels impossible now, but it isn't. You'll see in a few pages.

The catch? Once you have this amount saved up or you're on the path to saving it, you can't use it to pay off your debt or you'll be right back in that Stinky Cycle. Yes, this will cost you more money in interest. But (1) you must take care of yourself first, and (2) it's going to make you feel better. The key to this is balance.

When you otherwise would have borrowed from your credit card, you will instead now borrow from your savings account. You'll notice it becomes a lot more painful to part with your savings than it is to use a credit card and have to figure out how to pay it off later.

Workout #5.6: Prioritizing Your Priorities

Go back to your Spending Plan (Workout #5.4) one more time, look at where your money goes, and journal your way through these prompts.

* I can't live without...

* I could probably live without (but I'd rather not)...

* I could live without these things but I refuse to because I'm an adult, dammit...

* I can live without...

Be sure your spending plan, target date, and debt payoff reflect these priorities, and if they don't, keep shuffling them around until you have a plan that incorporates the things that will keep you happy, sane, and motivated. Revisit these at least once every six months to a year to be sure they are fresh, up to date, and authentically *you*.

Workout #5.7: Your Debt-Dominating Plan Summary

The beauty of a plan is in its simplicity. You have a target date and a certain amount of money to put toward your debt each month. Let's revisit the questions from Workout #5.1… now with real numbers!

Doing:

1. The total debt I have is $______________________.

2. I will pay it off by ______________________ (*date*), which is in

   ____________months.

3. I will put $______________________ toward my debt each month on top of the interest.

4. I will put $______________________ into savings each month.

5. When my debt is paid off, I will have $______________________ in savings.

Feeling:

* Some of the sacrifices I will have to make are…

* Some of the things I won't be sacrificing are…

* I think these things are going to be a challenge…

* I think these things are going to be easy…

* I am excited because…

Workout #5.8: Play Date!

YOU ARE AMAZING. This is it. Allllll the hard work of planning is done now! Go do something nice for yourself to celebrate! Then come back and we'll talk about implementing these plans.

For support and bonus resources to accompany these workouts, come hang out at **OweLessLiveMore.com**!

In this chapter we will...

- ✱ Conquer the thoughts, ideas, and behaviors that may trip you up as you implement your plans.
- ✱ Master the practical aspects of paying off your debt: keeping the money flowing, handling the logistics of paying, and staying on track to hit your goals.

Step Six: *implement*

What does it take to succeed at implementing your plans? My high school gym teacher said it best, albeit in a completely different context. As she demonstrated how to thwart an advancing opponent in basketball, she would shout:

"Don't panic—adjust!"

(Aside: I am hopeless at basketball and pretty much every other sport, too. But this sage wisdom really stuck with me!)

You may not hit your target date. You may spend more money than you intended. *Life* may happen and force you to re-evaluate your choices. If you slip, don't allow yourself to fall. It is all perfect. You have everything you need. Don't panic. Adjust.

Dominating your debt is, after all, a journey. Once you arrive at your destination, freedom from debt will be your new normal and you'll forget what you felt like in this moment. Oh, was *that* all I had to do?

If you have done the workouts, you are already in much better financial and emotional shape, but know that challenges will still come up as you go. Dominating your debt may mean busting out of familiar routines and embracing a new way of living, and it may mean yelling "HUSH UP" to the naysaying voices in your head telling you this is too hard, that you can't do it.

You *can*. This chapter is all about how.

The Inner Game: Defeating the Tricky Little B*tches

Inside your mind live tricky little b*tches who don't want you to feel powerful and in control of your debt. If paying off your debt were a figure-skating competition, your performance in these five key areas would determine your score:

1. **Motivation.**

Motivation keeps you getting up and going when your get up and go has got up and went. Your main motivation will come from those three big-picture goals you outlined in Workout #2.1. Those goals are really important, but they may also feel far away. Even more vital to your success is the series of micro-victories that happen day to day. Every time you make a choice that gets you one step closer to where you want to be, you'd better celebrate the *hell* out of it.

2. **Awareness.**

If you want to be in control, there is no such thing as blissful ignorance. About anything. How much is your debt costing you? How much can you put toward it? What needs to happen next? Pay close attention to every little thing, because every little thing is magnified exponentially by interest.

3. **Confidence.**

Want to become a smooth numbers operator? Get comfortable asking questions. Learn as much as you can. Lay your plans carefully. Sleep soundly on minor mistakes, knowing that they won't derail your whole operation. Confidence comes from experience. To use another driving comparison: the first time you ever tried to change lanes, you looked over your shoulder twenty times while screeching, "OMG can I go now? Can I go *now*? AHHHHHHH!" Now, you flick on your blinker, glance in the rearview mirror, and coolly and calmly move your car into the next lane. The same thing will happen with your debt. Keep at it, and this will get easier.

4. **Habits.**

Regardless of what got you into debt, getting out probably means doing things differently than you have been. What is your routine? What is familiar? Which of your structures, behaviors, and tendencies are serving you, and which do you need to kick to the curb so you can move forward? And with what are you going to replace them? We want to get you on autopilot so you can control your debt without thinking. If you have a significant amount of debt, you're in this for the long haul. It will be so much easier for you if you don't have to stress about it so damn much.

5. **Perception.**

You've been forming your relationship with money since the day it first impacted your life—which is to say, a really long time ago. If, like so many of my clients (before I got my hands on them!), you have accepted debt as inevitable, that thought didn't just appear out of nowhere. Your perception of debt is directly related to the role money has played in your life. Part of this journey is unraveling the wires that led to that perception and rerouting them in a way that serves you both financially and emotionally.

The Outer Game: Managing the Practical Affairs

Follow these six rules to stay on top of your numbers and ensure the inner game tricky little b*tches don't run the show.

1. **Be organized.**

Use the spreadsheets and charts in this book. I mean *really use them*. Make them a part of your life. Review and update them regularly. Money loves to be arranged in neat and tidy rows and columns. Does the thought of dealing with your numbers make you want to gouge out your eyeballs (even *after* reading this book)? Being organized will make it *so much less painful.*

2. **Be consistent.**

Have an "Admin Day" once a week, each week, on the same day. (You can dress it up and call it a "Money Date," but no matter the title, it's still going to feel pretty admin-y.) On this day, review and update your accounts, spreadsheets, charts, and the status of your debts.

Why once a week? Why every week? Why the same day? This weekly date with your money will help you develop a habit. One of the main characteristics of a habit is that you do it without thinking much about it. If Friday is your Admin Day, once you get in the habit you'll have very little to remember during the rest of the week. And if you do this every week, after the first few, it will take less time and feel less onerous because not much will have changed week to week, leaving you with fewer tasks on your to-do list.

3. **Be supported.**

You can do this alone, but why torture yourself? It will be infinitely more enjoyable if you're having a mini-party throughout the process. Figure out what kind of support you need and make it part of your plan to get it. Work with a financial coach and make sure you totally *rock* it. Join a Dominate Your Debt™ Boot Camp and enjoy the loving camaraderie of others going through the exact same thing as you. Find a friend or an accountability buddy who is as serious and savvy as you are about taking control. Talk to your family and close friends—even if they don't understand what you're going through, they may still be supportive. Money is a private thing, and I know being so exposed may feel strange or embarrassing at first, but I *promise* you that doing this alone, while totally possible, will suck way more than it needs to.

4. **Be kind.**

This is the #1 most important tip I can give you. Be kind to yourself. Don't be fooled into thinking this isn't a big deal, or berate yourself for not having done XYZABCD by now. Paying off debt is a big deal. It's a *huge* deal. And you should be incredibly, insanely, outrageously proud of yourself just for attempting this feat, let alone actually succeeding (which you will!). People die with their debt. You're determined not to. So if something goes awry, shake it off. *Who cares*? You can fix it. You have everything you need to fix it. Now cut yourself some slack and give yourself a hug.

5. **Have fun.**

I know I already said this, but I'm repeating it for emphasis: you're in this for the long haul. All work and no play… well, you know how that one ends. Treat your debt with the dignity it deserves *and* infuse your life with fun. Some suggestions:

- Post inspirational quotes or pictures of people whose awesomeness drives you around your mirror.
- Take dance breaks to songs that make you want to *move*.
- Go to a karaoke bar with few close friends, make a pact not to judge anyone, and sing like crazy.

- Write a letter to yourself about how awesome you are and mail it to yourself.
- Ask your friends and family to send you cards saying, "Hooray! You kick ass!"
- Write a love letter to your debt and hang it on your wall.
- Write a hate letter to your debt and burn it in a ceremonial pyre.
- Make a découpage folder to store all of your debt documents.
- Create a vision board to represent your "So I can..."s.
- Take up a physical hobby that will make you sweat and/or feel like a badass, such as running, kickboxing, swimming, or belly dancing.
- Take up a physical hobby that will calm and relax you, such as yoga or meditation.
- Visit your local library, explore the stacks at random, and borrow every book that interests or inspires you (they are all free!).

This is far from an exhaustive list. The point is, *don't live only for your debt.* Build fun into your schedule (and budget!). Find the things that really make your heart sing and *do them.*

6. **Reward your progress.**

While there are many emotional aspects to this process, dealing with debt ultimately involves numbers. Numbers are easy to manipulate and to track, but they aren't tangible.

To counter this, measure your progress in numbers *and* tie it to something concrete and fabulous. This will keep you motivated and give you a much more exciting incentive than looking at digits on a screen. Monitor and reward your progress. Get creative! It can be as simple as watching an old episode of *Friends* for every payment you make, or as ornate and visual as any of these:

- Print a big black and white poster and color a section for every chunk of debt you pay off.
- Write out each of your payments in bright, bold colors and cross them off one by one as you make them.

- Create a chart and give yourself a pretty sticker for every payment you make—you are never too mature for gold stars and smiley faces!

- Take a picture of yourself every month or each time you make a payment and paste it into a scrapbook or create a digital album; you will love the changes you see in yourself.

Having the Money

At the end of the day, all the motivation in the world won't mean a thing if the money isn't there. Only cash can make your debt go away. And the only two ways to create cash are to spend less and to bring in more. Here are some tips to accomplish each of these.

Spend Like You Mean It

If you need to spend less so you can free up more cash to throw at your debt, there are six main ways to do it.

1 *Cut waste.*

Cut waste, not joy. If stepping out to buy lunch is the best part of your day, then don't stress about not packing your lunch. But if you grab an expensive soup and salad because you didn't have time to make lunch at home because you went to bed too late because you were watching a TV show you don't even care about… you see what I'm saying? There's no judgment here. We just want you to be mindful and do your best to reserve your hard-earned money for the things that actually make you happy.

2. *Plan ahead.*

Planning in advance saves you money. You can shop sales, watch for deals, compare prices, etc. Impulse and last-minute purchases almost always cost more. When you go into a store to buy something, play a little game with yourself: have a number in mind and see what you can fit into that number.

3. *Avoid triggers.*

Once you've identified the stores or behaviors that are your triggers, I've got two words for you: *don't go*. Delete all your payment information from your online accounts so you have to seek out your card to pay. Don't go into stores where you always spend more than you intend to (this is me and Target!). It is normal to have triggers. Shifting habits takes determination and willpower. If you aren't sure you can control yourself, *just don't go*. Avoid certain temptation and give yourself space to recalibrate.

4. *Fall in love.*

While you're tackling your debt, everything that crosses the threshold into your home should be either something you *need* or something you *love*. For example, don't buy clothes that just fit. Buy clothes that *sing* on you. Before you put something into your shopping cart make sure it passes the three-question **Love Test**:

- Do I *love* this?
- Is this going to make me *so super happy*?
- Do I love this *more* than I would love to be free of my debt?

Buy only if you can answer "yes" to all three of these questions. Commit to asking and answering honestly, and respect your answers. You may be surprised!

5. *Focus on joy.*

Delight in activities big and small that don't cost anything. For activities you love that do cost money, scale back on how much or how often you do them. You don't have to stay home and wallow. Just make choices consciously. It's helpful if the people you roll with know what you're trying to achieve and support you totally—they are much more likely to encourage you than to interfere.

6. *Walk away.*

If you tend to impulse spend, this one is for you. When you shop, don't buy. Make a list of the things you saw and loved. Take the love test. Wait two more days before you purchase to see if the flames of love are still burning.

7. *Embrace treats.*

Yes. *Treat yourself.* There's nothing wrong with indulging! But let's be clear on what a treat is. A treat is something wonderful that is unexpected and/or happens once in a while. A habit, on the other hand, happens regularly and reflexively and doesn't have any particular emotions associated with it. Treats that have become habits are a source of big spending leaks for many people. Watch out for them. You can choose whatever treats or habits you want. Just be sure your choices are serving you and keeping you motivated rather than dragging you down.

Earn Like You Deserve It

Money comes from five main resources: your boss, your hustle, your stuff, your money, and your family. You can tap into any or all of these or others to create the cash to make your plan work.

1. *Your boss.*

Is it time for a raise? Approach your supervisor(s) armed with all the amazing things you've done and make your case.

2. *Your hustle.*

If you're allowed and have the energy, this may be the path of least resistance. You may have to swallow your pride and take a job or render a service for which you feel overqualified, but it can also be easy. (While I was a practicing attorney, I got a side job doing medical billing and bookkeeping because it was easy, steady money and I was damn good at it!) For the entrepreneurs and budding entrepreneurs out there, be sure that your hustle does not cost you more money than you will create.

3. *Your stuff.*

If you have nice clothes, shoes, equipment, electronics, etc. you may be able to sell them. Your resources are as unique as you are. When you've identified your priorities you won't feel (as much) like your choices are sacrifices.

4. *Your money.*

Money makes you money in two ways: (1) when you don't pay interest on it, and (2) when it grows and earns interest. One of the most obvious ways to create money to pay off debt is—you guessed it!—to pay off debt. As your principal balance decreases, so will your minimum payment and interest charges.

5. *Your family.*

Whether and to what extent you can ask your family for financial assistance with your debt will depend on your relationship with your family, their own financial situation, and whether you feel comfortable going to them for help.

The Logistics of Making Payments

Here is how to navigate the most common challenges when paying down your credit cards and federal student loans:

Paying Down Your Credit Cards

It is difficult to pay off credit card debt while you are still using the card(s). For that reason, I highly recommend you either (a) switch to a debit card until your credit card debt is completely paid off, or (b) start using a new credit card and treat it like a debit card, meaning you never, ever charge more than you can afford to pay in full by the end of the billing cycle. If you must use the same card on which you are carrying debt, pay off all new purchases in full before your due date.

If, even with your spending plan, Admin Day, and cash tracking, you are concerned about keeping tabs on what goes in and out of your bank account, a pre-loaded debit card may be a good option for you.

If you are using your credit card to support yourself because your expenses are higher than what you make each month, you *must* find a way to create more money if you want to take control of your debt. I wish I had better news for you, but there is nothing magical about this part. If you want to get ahead of your debt, you must buy less than you can afford with your earnings in a given month.

Credit Card FAQs

How do I know what amount to pay?

When you make a payment toward your credit card, you have three choices: current balance, statement balance, and minimum payment. Unless your current balance happens to be lower, the only number that matters is the statement balance. As long as you pay your statement balance in full on or before the due date, you will never pay interest. You do not have to zero out the current balance to avoid interest.

Should I close my card once I've paid it off?

Once you've paid off a card, you may be itching to close it so that you won't be tempted to use it anymore. Don't! Keep your cards open. Closing cards can damage your credit score because it reduces the amount of credit you have available and shortens your credit history. Hide them, cut them up, leave them at home, and definitely monitor them for fraud... but don't close them.

Paying Down Your Federal Student Loans

Here's how to dominate the process of paying extra towards your federal student loans.

Make sure extra money gets applied to your principal.

When paying extra (i.e., more than the minimum payment) toward your federal student loans, your lender will give you two options as to how to apply that payment:

1. Apply extra to your next payment and advance your due date.

2. Apply extra to principal and don't advance your due date.

Unless you have a very specific reason otherwise, you *always* want the option that will **apply extra to principal and not advance your due date**.

The first option, "advance your due date," means "no payments will be due next month." This may seem like an attractive option—yay, no payment next month!—but it's not helping you pay off your debt sooner at all. Next month, you pay nothing. The month after that, you resume payments and nothing has changed.

The second option, "apply to principal and don't advance your due date," is the one you want. Next month your required minimum payment will be less than it was this month. The term of your debt will be shortened. You will charged less interest because you have lowered the principal. And if you can continue to make your original higher minimum payment and apply all the extra to principal each month, you will start to see your balance go down a *lot* faster.

Note: Every student loan website is different, so you may have to poke around quite a bit to locate the "apply to principal" option, and it may not be worded exactly this way. Take the time to find it. If the default option is the "advance your due date" option, you'll have a heck of a time trying to claw the money back and apply it the way you want. If you must pay by check, include a letter with clear instructions and write those instructions in the memo portion of the check as well. Once you make the payment, keep checking back to make sure it was correctly applied.

Remember the interest!

Remember: (1) your student loans accrue interest every day, and (2) payments are applied first to fees, then to interest, then to principal. By the time your payment hits your account, your balance will have increased. For example, say you put an extra $1,000 toward your student loan principal. Some of the $1,000 will be sucked up by the interest that has accrued since the day you made your payment, so your principal will not be reduced by exactly $1,000.

Most student loan sites have a calculator that will tell you how much interest will accrue three to ten days out so that you can adjust your extra payment accordingly. This is especially important in the event you're paying off an entire loan.

Be specific when paying off individual loans.

If your loans are lumped together under one account with one minimum payment that is applied to several loans, you will have to specify to which loan you want your payment applied or else your loan company will apply it equally to all payments. This is important if you identified one of your loans as a higher priority and want to make sure your payment goes to that one first. Some student loan providers have a separate "pay" button for each individual loan, and some don't. If you aren't able to pay off your loans the way you want to, don't be afraid to get someone on the phone and keep asking for supervisors until someone understands what you want to do and can help you do it.

Paying Everything Else

As you pay for things, whether a phone bill or a salad from the neighborhood deli, you must hold yourself accountable. This means tracking everything you spend. Once a week, on your Admin Day, download your expenditures from your credit or debit card activity into a table or spreadsheet. Really do this each week; if you don't, not only will it *feel* like an icky, arduous task, it will actually *be* an icky, arduous task. If you want to be aware and accountable, know that every dollar you spend is one you will have to face later when you see it on your statement and enter it into your spreadsheet.

Pay bills a few days before they're due. You won't forget; the Admin Day schedule will ensure you stay on top of everything. You don't get brownie points for paying bills early, so if your goal is to dominate your debt, just stay current and focus on your debt.

Pre-Payment Penalties

This is very rare, as many states have outlawed this practice, but it bears mentioning. Be *sure* there is no penalty associated with paying off your debt early. Look for this information in the fine print or call your lender directly. It may come in the form of a fee, or a bill for the total amount of interest that would have been due over the lifetime of the original term.

Paying Yourself

We talked about the importance of balancing savings with paying off debt. There are various ways to do this. Here is the one I recommend.

The key is three accounts—two savings accounts and (at least) one retirement or investment account.

1. One regular savings account linked to your checking account.
   - Put money into this account until it contains approximately one extra month of living expenses.
   - Most people don't need huge buffers in their checking accounts, and your life savings definitely does not belong there, either!
2. One online high-interest savings account to which your checking account is linked as an external account.
   - This is where you build your fluffy Snug-as-a-Bug mattress.
   - Money goes in to this account but it does not come out!
3. One retirement account that is *actually invested* in something.
   - Ask your human resources department or a financial adviser to help you set this up.

Step Six Workouts: Implement

I commit to doing these workouts on [date(s)]: ______________________________

Workout #6.1: Admin Day

Decide on your Admin Day. Put it in your calendar. Set it as a recurring appointment and put a little smiley face next to it. You're awesome!

- My Admin Day is: ____________________
- I chose this day because…
- I am committed to sticking to this day because…
- Here are the things I will do to make this easy:

Workout #6.2: Track It, Baby

When you are out for total debt domination you need to track all your spending. The purpose of this is twofold: (1) to become deeply conscious of where your money goes, and (2) to be accountable to yourself for it. Every week on your Admin Day, fill in this chart with the details—date, what was purchased, the amount, and the category—of everything on which you spent money that week.

This is why using a card—whether debit, credit, or pre-loaded debit—is crucial. If you use cash you will have to contend with receipts and your memory, neither of which is going to make this feel easy for you.

Keep a running total, a monthly total, a weekly total, or all three.

Don't hate me! You will not need to do this from now until the end of time. This is designed to recalibrate you, to make you acutely aware of your spending and how it impacts your relationship with your debt. This will also help you recognize patterns and triggers in your spending. Use the notes column to jot down how you were feeling that day, or how you feel about that particular outflow now.

Spending Tracker

DATE	MONEY OUT	CATEGORY	NOTES

Spending Tracker, Continued

DATE	MONEY OUT	CATEGORY	NOTES

Workout #6.3: Savings Sandbox

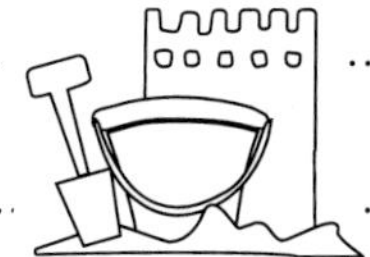

It's a tired cliché, but when it comes to saving you really do need to pay yourself first. Otherwise, there's a high probability that you won't save at all, and a near certainty that you won't save with any level of consistency. The easiest way to save is to set up an automatic transfer into your savings account to coordinate with the day after you receive your paycheck.

How much to save? You've already computed your Snug-as-a-Bug number (and it may feel very daunting and huge, particularly if you aren't anywhere close to that right now). Savings is one of the clearest illustrations of the idea that *small changes yield big results over time.*

> **Example:** Your Snug-as-a-Bug number is $5,000. If you save $100 a month, or $50 from every biweekly paycheck, you will hit your Snug-as-a-Bug number sometime between Years 4 and 5.
>
> Increasing that number by $50 a month, or $12.50 a week, will give you $150 per month. You won't notice a big difference at first, but you definitely will when you hit your target Snug-as-a-Bug savings number between Years 2 and 3 and have almost double that target number by Year 5!

Here's a chart to really hit this point home. (I'll give you the example first, and then it will be your turn!) At first, the difference between the two accounts is negligible, but over time there's a pretty big gap. Which is why it's really important to stay the course!

Savings Sandbox

	$100 PER MONTH ($25 PER WEEK)	$150 PER MONTH ($37.50 PER WEEK)	DIFFERENCE
Month 1	$100.00	$150.00	$50.00
Month 2	$200.00	$300.00	$100.00
Month 3	$300.00	$450.00	$150.00
Month 4	$400.00	$600.00	$200.00
Month 5	$500.00	$750.00	$250.00
Month 6	$600.00	$900.00	$300.00
Month 7	$700.00	$1,050.00	$350.00
Month 8	$800.00	$1,200.00	$400.00
Month 9	$900.00	$1,350.00	$450.00
Month 10	$1,000.00	$1,500.00	$500.00
Month 11	$1,100.00	$1,650.00	$550.00
Month 12	$1,200.00	$1,800.00	$600.00
Year 2 (Month 24)	$2,400.00	$3,600.00	$1,200.00
Year 3 (Month 36)	$3,600.00	**$5,400.00**	$1,800.00
Year 4 (Month 48)	$4,800.00	$7,200.00	$2,400.00
Year 5 (Month 60)	**$6,000.00**	$9,000.00	$3,000.00

Now it's your turn to play in the Savings Sandbox! Try different numbers. See what resonates and how soon you can hit your goals. This is just an estimate that assumes your financial situation will be exactly the same in five years, which of course it probably won't. A lot can change and hopefully it will be even better! This workout isn't designed to predict the future. It is a window into what's possible.

Savings Sandbox

	$______PER MONTH ($______PERWEEK)	$______PER MONTH ($______PER WEEK)	DIFFERENCE
Month 1			
Month 2			
Month 3			
Month 4			
Month 5			
Month 6			
Month 7			
Month 8			
Month 9			
Month 10			
Month 11			
Month 12			
Year 2 (Month 24)			
Year 3 (Month 36)			
Year 4 (Month 48)			
Year 5 (Month 60)			

Workout #6.4: Your Balanced Payoff Plan

This is it! It's finally time to create a payoff plan that balances building savings with paying off debt.

You will start by noting four things:

1. Your total debt.
2. Your savings goal.
3. The total amount you have available each month to put toward savings and debt.
4. How you want to split that total amount between paying off debt and building savings.

From there, you will build out your balanced payoff plan. We'll start with a couple of examples and then you'll have a blank chart to complete with your own numbers.

Example:

1. Your total debt: $10,000.00
2. Your savings goal: $5,000.00
3. Total amount available to put toward savings and debt each month: $1,000.00
4. How to split between debt and savings:

   Debt payment amount: $850.00

   Savings amount: $150.00

	SAVINGS BUILD-UP	DEBT PAY-DOWN
Start	$0.00	$10,000.00
Month 1	$150.00	$9,150.00
Month 2	$300.00	$8,300.00
Month 3	$450.00	$7,450.00
Month 4	$600.00	$6,600.00
Month 5	$750.00	$5,750.00
Month 6	$900.00	$4,900.00
Month 7	$1,050.00	$4,050.00
Month 8	$1,200.00	$3,200.00
Month 9	$1,350.00	$2,350.00
Month 10	$1,500.00	$1,500.00
Month 11	$1,650.00	$650.00
Month 12 (Year 1)	$1,800.00	**-$200.00**
Month 13	$2,800.00	DEBT PAID OFF!
Month 14	$3,800.00	
Month 15	$4,800.00	
Month 16	**$5,800.00**	SAVINGS GOAL HIT!
Month 17	$6,800.00	
Month 18	$7,800.00	
Month 19	$8,800.00	
Month 20	$9,800.00	
Month 21	$10,800.00	
Month 22	$11,800.00	
Month 23	$12,800.00	
Month 24 (Year 2)	$13,800.00	
Month 36 (Year 3)	$25,800.00	WOW!!!

If these were your numbers, your entire debt will have been paid off by Month 12! Once the debt is gone, if you started putting the whole available amount toward savings, you'd hit your $5,000 savings goal in Month 16... and from there build some serious cash over the course of 36 months, or 3 years.

Here's another example, and then it will be your turn!

Example:

1. Your total debt: $10,000.00
2. Your savings goal: $5,000.00
3. Total amount available each month: $500.00
4. How to split between debt and savings:

   Debt payment amount: $400.00

   Savings amount: $100.00

	SAVINGS BUILD-UP	DEBT PAY-DOWN
Start	$0.00	$10,000.00
Month 1	$100.00	$9,600.00
Month 2	$200.00	$9,200.00
Month 3	$300.00	$8,800.00
Month 4	$400.00	$8,400.00
Month 5	$500.00	$8,000.00
Month 6	$600.00	$7,600.00
Month 7	$700.00	$7,200.00
Month 8	$800.00	$6,800.00
Month 9	$900.00	$6,400.00
Month 10	$1,000.00	$6,000.00
Month 11	$1,100.00	$5,600.00
Month 12 (Year 1)	$1,200.00	$5,200.00
Month 24 (Year 2)	$2,400.00	$400.00
Month 25	$2,500.00	**$0.00**
Month 26	$3,000.00	
Month 27	$3,500.00	
Month 28	$4,000.00	
Month 29	$4,500.00	
Month 30	**$5,000.00**	
Month 36 (Year 3)	$8,000.00	

Even with $500 available—half as much as in the previous example—if these were your numbers, you'd be able to pay off your $10,000 debt in two years, with $2,500 saved, and by the end of Year 3, you would have been able to save $8,000!

Now, it's your turn to play! Try different scenarios. Dream about what's possible, and think in real numbers. If you want or need more space to model this out, use a separate page or a spreadsheet.

1. My total debt: $________________.

2. My savings goal: $________________.

3. Total amount available each month to put toward savings and debt: $______ .

4. How to split between paying off debt and building savings:

   * Debt payment amount: $________________.

   * Savings amount: $________________.

The Math (easy + very doable!)

* In the savings column, add the savings amount to the number in the row directly above.

* In the debt pay-down column, subtract the debt payment amount from the number in the row directly above.

My Balanced Payoff Plan!

	SAVINGS BUILD-UP	DEBT PAY-DOWN
Start		
Month 1		
Month 2		
Month 3		
Month 4		
Month 5		
Month 6		
Month 7		
Month 8		
Month 9		
Month 10		
Month 11		
Month 12 (Year 1)		
Month 13		
Month 14		
Month 15		

My Balanced Payoff Plan!

	SAVINGS BUILD-UP	DEBT PAY-DOWN
Month 16		
Month 17		
Month 18		
Month 19		
Month 20		
Month 21		
Month 22		
Month 23		
Month 24 (Year 2)		
Month 25		
Month 26		
Month 27		
Month 28		
Month 29		
Month 30		
Month 31		

My Balanced Payoff Plan, Continued

	SAVINGS BUILD-UP	DEBT PAY-DOWN
Month 32		
Month 33		
Month 34		
Month 35		
Month 36 (Year 3)		
Month 48 (Year 4)		
Month 60 (Year 5)		
Month 72 (Year 6)		
Month 84 (Year 7)		
Month 96 (Year 8)		
Month 108 (Year 9)		
Month 120 (Year 10)		

Workout #6.5: FUN!

This is your last workout, and the most important.

How are you going to take care of yourself, stay inspired, reward yourself, track your progress, and make sure that you feel joy throughout this process?

This is *not* a to-do list, but rather a place for you to doodle and dream.

For support and bonus resources to accompany these workouts, come hang out at **OweLessLiveMore.com**!

Conclusion

The Journey

There are a lot of pages in this book, and you've just about read them all. We've figured out what you have, what you could have, what you will have, and how to make it happen.

Here's what I hope you now know in your bones:

1. To feel in control of your debt, you need a plan.
2. To implement your plan, you need money.
3. To have money, you need to spend less than you can afford.
4. To spend less than what you can afford, you need to commit.

Guess what? You've read an entire work and play book about debt. *You know how to commit.*

As you embark on this journey, your efforts may not feel like they're making a difference, particularly at first. Stay the course. Use the tips and strategies in Step 6. If you get knocked down, get up again.

Don't panic. Adjust.

The Mission

When I paid off my own debt, I didn't have this book. I was doing all the research on my own and piecing together the sordid details. Every new bit of information was like peeling a layer from a rotten onion. I felt duped and helpless. I wanted desperately to be in control.

I created a lot of the charts and tools I've shared with you in this book, and I asked myself many of the same questions I've asked you. Getting a grip on my situation didn't change it, but I understood that I had power. I knew what I needed to do. From that point it was just a question of doing it.

When life interfered with my plans, I freaked out, and then I revised my plans. I followed my heart and honored my top priorities (e.g., travel, my wedding, saying yes to fun experiences with friends and family) and put others (e.g., leaving my job) on hold. I celebrated my progress. I found my Snug-as-a-Bug savings number, and once I hit it, I put everything else toward my loans. I created my own payoff strategy, which involved (to varying degrees) consolidating, refinancing, deferring, forbearing, and choosing the order that would cost me as little interest as possible. As I chipped away at the principal, I found that I just didn't *want* other things as badly as I wanted to be rid of the burden of my debt.

While most of my lawyer colleagues lived in Manhattan and Brooklyn, I left Brooklyn and moved to Queens (which, while much cheaper, honestly wasn't much of a sacrifice—I love Queens). When my husband and I got married, we could have afforded an apartment with two bedrooms, but we settled comfortably in an apartment with one. I got a lot more selective with clothes shopping. I took on a variety of non-legal odd jobs—including bookkeeping, teaching voice lessons, and hosting karaoke—to make extra money.

I also asked my family for help. Every Christmas, every holiday, every birthday, I had only one response to the "what should we get you?" question: "Money for my student loans." Would it have made more sense to have asked for help to pay tuition from the outset rather than to pay off loans? Without a doubt. But, like so many of my clients and law school classmates, I truly did not grasp the impact the amount I was borrowing would have on my life.

Paying off my debt in full took five years. Granted, five years may sound impressive given the size of my debt, but five years is still a really long time to maintain a commitment like that. Maybe for you it will be less, or maybe it will take you even longer.

The sooner you can start, the sooner it will be over.

I also want to be clear: being in control of your debt, or even paying it off, is not the same as living debt-free forever. When people tell me sanctimoniously that they have never had debt, I just want to snap back, "Humph!"

Those people are rare, and you don't need to strive to be one of them. The goal is not to avoid debt. The goal is to be in control of debt and give it the attention and respect it deserves.

Even though my own scary, stressful student loan debt is paid off now, I'm still on a mission. I wrote this book for you because I believe owing someone money should not be fraught with so many unknowns and so much anxiety. You deserve better. We all deserve better.

You have everything you need now. "Better" is just around the bend.

You've got this.

Keep It Rockin'

I said this at the beginning, and now that we're at the end it bears repeating: if you've read this through but didn't get to do any of the workouts, that's OK. Let it percolate. When you're ready, come back to them. You can't dominate your debt by reading. You have to actually do it.

Get support. Use the tips and strategies in Chapter 6 to help you stay motivated and on track. Get your hands on the bonus resources that accompany this book at **OweLessLiveMore.com**. Enroll in a Dominate Your Debt™ Boot Camp and start kicking ass and taking names with other awesome women just like you. And please feel free to reach out to me at and tell me about your debt-dominating progress—I'd love to connect with you, cheer you on, and hear about your successes!

Acknowledgments

My cup, as they say, runneth over; this is a small expression of my gratitude and appreciation for those who helped bring this book to life. I am a proud advocate of finding the right support and by golly, I live what I preach. If dominating your debt takes a village, writing a book about it takes an entire city.

To the women I've had the great honor to call clients, I am humbled by your faith and trust in me. Hiring a financial coach is no insignificant act. It took me almost thirteen years and an expensive couple of degrees to find work I love, and it never feels like work because of you.

To all those who have guided and cheered me on, even in the earliest stages when this crazy adventure was just a glimmer of an idea (the list goes on forever; these are merely some of the highlights): René, Mary Anne, Cecelia, Sam, Lis, Lia, Jacquie, Neha, Parag, Kerry, Gretchen, Elisha, Dave, Amy, Vijay, Erin, Meisan, Lucas, Cindy, Chris, Michelle, Marli, Chris, Lindsay, Anne, Kim, Sarah, Trenia, Danielle, and most especially the girlfriends who are my family: Allie, Aysha, Deepa, Heather, Holli, Isabelle, Merry, Naomi, and Sara. I love you all and I couldn't have done this without you.

To Holli (again), for the late nights and legal pads filled with scribbles, for book clubs, brunches, Broadway, beaches, and dark basement bars. East Coast, West Coast, doesn't matter… you always know just how to make sh*t happen. A million thanks.

To Justin, Anik, Louis, and Kim, for allowing me to pepper you with legal questions and answering every single one in exquisite detail, with patience and grace.

To Kristen, for telling me to *go* rather than sit and think too hard, to Farideh for being my virtual shoulder to cry on, and to Stella for making smart look hot.

To Joe, Karin, Krylyn, Linda, and Liz, for sharing your thoughts, comments, perspectives, and contributions.

To Eminem, whose music provided me with both the soundtrack to this book and motivation on the days when the only way I could get down to business was hearing him say it first.

To the rockstar team at Union Park Press and Fyfe Design for their hard work and dedication to excellence: Nicole, Bryn, Caitlin, Erin and of course my stunningly talented editor Deepa. Words cannot express how grateful I am for your enthusiasm and commitment to me and to this project. Without you this book never would have been written; I'm sure of that. And Deepa… Magic happens when we work together. I'm so lucky and so happy (times infinity!) to still have you in my life.

To Kim, my biz BFF, for your thoughtfulness, generosity, and genius, and for introducing me to *Scandal*. Thank you for holding tight to my dreams.

To Therese, my incredible mentor, coach, and soul mama; to my Red Hot sisters Katie, Leah, and Leslie; and to the women at the springtime retreat in Arizona. You are, collectively, a powerful force of resilience and determination. You helped me surrender to the whisperings of my soul, gave me permission, and wrapped me in love. I am grateful every day that we found each other.

To Mama L, thank you for treating me like I was your daughter, too. I owe you so much and miss you even more.

To Sharon and Raff, I'm so glad we have each other. Thank you for being my family.

To my mom, who taught me to love books, to my dad, who taught me to laugh, and to both my parents… thank you for always believing in me and making me feel I could do anything. I hope I've done you proud.

To Jon, my angel, for your love, encouragement, patience, laughter, and graphic design skills, for spoiling me silly, and for making marriage feel easy. To Baxter, for snuggles and distractions; how can so much happiness be packed into six furry little pounds? To my daughter, for already being so strong and fearless and sweet… one day you will read this and I hope you will be proud your mom wrote it. I love you.

And finally, to my grandparents, Bob and Yvette, my Mémé and Pépé. This book is for you; everything in here was born of your wisdom, support, faith, and unconditional love. I wish I could send you the ten copies I know you would have wanted. You are and always have been my inspiration, and I know I'm blessed to have had so many opportunities to tell you so. I love you loads and I miss you. Thank you for always making sure I knew how much I was loved.

To every person who reads this book, does the workouts, and learns the tools they need to take control: I have done a trust fall, and you have caught me. I hope I can catch you right back.

Thank you from the bottom of my bursting heart.

....

Rebecca Eve Selkowe is on a mission to empower all women to be confident and in control of their money. She earned her B.A., *magna cum laude*, from Middlebury College and her J.D. from Brooklyn Law School.

As a financial coach, Rebecca has been featured in Yahoo! Finance and The Story Exchange and is a sought-after speaker and trainer on the subjects of financial fitness and empowerment.

An award-winning karaoke performer (yes, this is a thing!), Rebecca lives in New York City with the three loves of her life: her husband, her daughter, and her six-pound Maltipoo.

You can find her at OweLessLiveMore.com.

....